The Story of Rena Stewart

The Story of Rena Stewart

Bletchley Park Girl, Translator of Hitler's Will, and BBC Pioneer

Victoria Walsh

First published in Great Britain in 2025 by
Pen & Sword History
An imprint of Pen & Sword Books Limited
Yorkshire – Philadelphia

Copyright © Victoria Walsh 2025

ISBN 978 1 03613 390 0

The right of Victoria Walsh to be identified as
Author of this Work has been asserted by her in accordance
with the Copyright, Designs and Patents Act 1988.

A CIP catalogue record for this book is
available from the British Library.

All rights reserved. No part of this book may be reproduced, transmitted, downloaded, decompiled or reverse engineered in any form or by any means, electronic or mechanical including photocopying, recording or by any information storage and retrieval system, without permission from the Publisher in writing. NO AI TRAINING: Without in any way limiting the Author's and Publisher's exclusive rights under copyright, any use of this publication to "train" generative artificial intelligence (AI) technologies to generate text is expressly prohibited. The Author and Publisher reserve all rights to license uses of this work for generative AI training and development of machine learning language models.

Typeset by Mac Style
Printed in the UK by CPI Group (UK) Ltd, Croydon, CR0 4YY.

The Publisher's authorised representative in the EU for product safety is Authorised Rep Compliance Ltd., Ground Floor, 71 Lower Baggot Street, Dublin D02 P593, Ireland.
www.arccompliance.com

For a complete list of Pen & Sword titles please contact

PEN & SWORD BOOKS LIMITED
47 Church Street, Barnsley, South Yorkshire, S70 2AS, England
E-mail: enquiries@pen-and-sword.co.uk
Website: www.pen-and-sword.co.uk
or
PEN AND SWORD BOOKS
1950 Lawrence Road, Havertown, PA 19083, USA
E-mail: uspen-and-sword@casematepublishers.com
Website: www.penandswordbooks.com

To Rena, with thanks for your service to your country,
and for cracking a few glass ceilings!

'My greatest achievement has been getting people to recognise that a woman can be as good a journalist as a man.'
Rena Stewart, 17 February 1923 to 11 November 2023

Photographs provided by Rena's nephew and executor, Stewart Maclennan, unless otherwise stated.

Contents

Family Foreword ix
Professional Foreword xi
Introduction xiii

Part One: Rena's Story 1

1	A Splendid Scottish Start to Life	3
2	St Andrews: Best Years and Bombs	6
3	Signing Up: Silk or Khaki?	8
4	Basic Training: Ranks and Rifles	9
5	Officially Secret	10
6	Bletchley Beginnings	11
7	The German Book Room	13
8	Park Life	20
9	Keeping the Secret	27
10	Demob Deferred	29
11	The Epic Journey to Germany	30
12	Bad Nenndorf: Back to Work	34
13	A Top-secret Task	38
14	Life and Love in Post-war Germany	43
15	Homewards	46
16	At the BBC, from the Bottom Up	47
17	Caversham Monitoring Station: Progress and Peril	50
18	Into the Newsroom	52
19	Senior Duty Editor, *and* a Woman!	54
20	On Marriage (and Cracking Glass Ceilings)	56
21	Time Out	57
22	Retirement	58
23	Back to Bletchley	60
24	Songs (and Dances) of Praise	62
25	A Significant Celebration	64
26	A Significant Achievement	65

| 27 | Creature Comforts | 66 |
| 28 | … and a Celebration of a Life Well Lived | 67 |

Part Two: Remembering Rena's Bletchley Friends — 69

1	Agnes Glynn (née Gardner)	71
2	Elma Wasmoeth (née Morley)	74
3	Margery Tarwinska (née Forbes)	77

Part Three: Three Mysteries — 79

Mystery One: Bill, Hugh, and Hitler's Wills — 81

1	The Mystery	82
2	Bill	84
3	Hugh	86
4	Hitler's Wills	92
5	The Investigation	96
6	The Book	101
7	The Translation	102
8	… and Back to Bill	104

Mystery Two: The Missing German Book Room — 107

1	The Mystery	108
2	The Investigation	109
3	The Conclusion	113

Mystery Three: Missiles and Monitoring — 115

1	The Mystery	116
2	The Investigation	118
3	The Conclusion	120

Acknowledgements — 121
Notes — 123
Bibliography — 134
Index — 138

Family Foreword

In an age of shallow and spurious 'celebrity', my aunt Rena Stewart's life is truly worthy of celebration, from her arrival in the world in 1923, as a late addition to her family and sister to my mother, Isobel. Both took their acute intelligence to university: Isobel to Edinburgh, Rena to St Andrews.

The barriers confronting ambitious young women in the 1930s are scarcely comprehensible today. Only a tiny proportion attained university; there, they were often denied full qualification. Women seeking to combine a career with marriage were barred frequently, not only by social convention but by legal enforcement; an iniquity which befell my mother's teaching career. Set against these handicaps, Rena's early determination to be a journalist might seem an improbable fancy.

Her iron will made fancy reality, but first, there was the matter of duty in the war against fascism. Equipped with outstanding language qualifications, Rena volunteered for service and was posted to the Bletchley Park de-coding centre. Then this 'modern Amazon' (warrior woman), as she described herself, tongue in cheek, undertook translation work at the Bad Nenndorf interrogation unit near Hanover. Her distinguished service at both were shrouded for many years, by security restrictions and by Rena's own modesty.

Returning to civilian life in 1947, Rena pursued a dream deferred. Debarred from disclosing her significant wartime role, she hammered at the door of the BBC until she gained grudging admittance, initially only as a clerk in the World Service. She pressed again and again, until successful, for posts commensurate with her remarkable talents. Against all odds, Rena rose to become the World Service's first woman senior duty editor, in a (second) working career spanning 36 years.

Rena was the linchpin of her family, thinking nothing of undertaking journeys of several hundred miles to the West Highlands to visit her sister and infant nephew. When that same nephew reached his teens, his holidays were often taken with an aunt whose cultural sophistication and vitality transformed his education. Rena encouraged and informed his early interest in history and politics, believing in and embodying responsible and engaged citizenship, and an outlook which transcended national boundaries.

Following retirement in 1983, Rena was joined by her sister Isobel, now widowed, and together this formidable sisterhood set up a new home in Ealing, west London. 'Compulsive joiners', they were active and generous participants in local social life, bringing also their special interests in Scottish heritage, country dancing and traditional music. They became worshippers at St Andrews United Reformed Church, befitting the daughters of a church organist and elder for nearly 50 years. They pursued their mutual love of travel energetically, as regular and much-loved guests on National Trust cruises.

As public interest in the wartime role of Bletchley Park grew, so too did recognition of its crucial role in the Allied victory. Rena's energies now embraced the promotion of the Bletchley Park Trust, serving as a guide and honoured as a veteran, her name standing proud on Bletchley's Roll of Honour.

Both Isobel and Rena would be beneficiaries of the famed longevity of the Williamson women in our family: Isobel passed away aged 90 in 2004; Rena lived on at full pace to achieve her centenary and break the family record. A fall in her latter years greatly restricted her mobility, but she lived and died in her own home, supported by friends, neighbours and carers.

In February 2023 Rena attained her centenary, with a joyous gathering at the deconsecrated medieval church of St Mary's Perivale, a place she loved, sponsored and supported for many years. Later in her last year, great good fortune arrived in the form of a young author who sensitively began the long-overdue work of setting down Rena's fascinating life story. Rena's unique voice rings clear and true in Victoria's telling.

To the end, Rena began her day by scrutinising *The Times* and *The Guardian* with a fine editorial eye. She would have been delighted that both would offer prominent and generous obituaries, and she would be astonished to find a similar tribute in Italy's *La Stampa*.

She now rests, with her mother and father at Largo Parish Church in Fife, Scotland, her long life led with passion and commitment, grace and distinction.

By Stewart Maclennan (Rena's nephew)

Professional Foreword

Newsrooms in the 1970s were largely male dominated. BBC World Service – then known as External Services – was no exception. It was a very serious and dedicated place but, at the same time, a boys' club: boozy, noisy, sweary and full of men who had learned their trade in the print media. Many had served in the Forces. If you were female, you weren't popular. If you weren't from the print media, you weren't popular, and if you were a university graduate, you weren't popular. The few women coped with all this masculinity in different ways. Some were compliant, some were indifferent, and some attempted to be 'one of the boys'.

And then there was Rena. Rena was duty editor when I joined the Newsroom in 1973 or 4 – a person of considerable power. Bruised by my encounters with some of the more vocal and critical male journalists, she was a revelation. To start with, she listened, head cocked in that familiar way. Her voice, with its pleasing Scottish burr, was always gentle. She never, in all the time I knew her, lost her temper, but if she was displeased, people knew it. She was very calm, very tactful and quite determined to get her own way, which she did. There was no arguing with her!

Rena soon became an SDE – a senior duty editor. This was the person who was in charge of the newsroom on any given shift. The SDE commissions the stories and dispatches, dictates the headlines and makes sure that the news gets on the air. And in those days, we were broadcasting in 42 languages. Rena was the first woman to achieve this post. I can see her now, sitting at that SDE's desk, with her gentle smile and will of iron!

Rena was terrific: kind, gentle, funny, imaginative, supremely confident, and what was known as a safe pair of hands. She was, above all, a consummate journalist. Her wartime experience at Bletchley Park had given her a good commitment to the sources (that is, always drawing on multiple sources). Nothing got past her. She had an analytical mind and, dealing with the sorts of stories we had, she was unlocking mysteries all the time. She was so highly thought of that when the World Service left Bush House, Rena was called in to preside over the very last bulletin.

She was also a leading light for a lot of us. My generation of women journalists realised that the more senior jobs were not beyond their reach, and I began to see that there was a place for me in that newsroom.

And at the end of a long career, I can only say 'Thank you, Rena!'

By Sally-Anne Thomas (a former colleague of Rena and senior duty editor at the BBC). Note from the author: I was very sorry to hear that Sally-Anne (Sally to her family) died in July 2024, but I was grateful for her input.

Introduction

'You *must* meet my next-door neighbour. She's 100 years old, a Bletchley Park Girl, and she's just starting to lose her memory … but she's keen to talk'. This invitation, from a family friend, Jan Harrison, is how I came to meet the wonderful Rena Stewart, in June 2023. Time was ticking, so I agreed immediately, and I'm so glad I did. I just hadn't thought that her story would become a book, but as it turned out, she was seriously interesting!

Rena Williamson Robertson Stewart was an ordinary but extraordinary Scotswoman who celebrated her centenary in 2023. Rena (pronounced Reena) was a 'Bletchley Park Girl' who went on to translate Hitler's will and to blaze a trail for women at the BBC. This book tells Rena's life story, which I hope you will find as fascinating as I do. This is followed by a short biography of each of her three best Bletchley friends: Agnes Glynn (née Gardner), Elma Wasmoeth (née Morley) and Margery Tarwinska (née Forbes). In addition, at the end of the book there are three small historical mysteries that arose from Rena's story. These relate to Bletchley Park, Hitler's will and the BBC.

Although Rena's memory was fading, I assumed that I'd have longer with her. Unfortunately, she fell ill and died suddenly, on 11 November 2023 (Armistice Day). However, she had seen an early draft of the book and given it her blessing. She died before I could ask her all the questions I'd have liked to, and there were some that she didn't know the answer to. For example, was she involved in resolving the Cuban Missile Crisis while working at the BBC World Service? Curious, I went off sleuthing. My investigations eventually became a big part of the book – especially the story of Bill Oughton and Hugh Trevor-Roper, two intelligence officers linked to Rena's translation of Hitler's will.

It was a huge privilege to meet Rena, and to hear about her life. She was a humble person but determined, and with a good sense of humour. My first visit coincided with a heat wave, and half way through, I checked with her to see if she had enough energy to carry on. Without hesitation, she replied: 'Oh of course, I'm always happy to blether about myself'.

I've written Rena's biography in the first person, and in her manner of speaking. I've also tried hard to fill in the many gaps in her story. I've added comments, information and historical corrections (in square brackets and grey boxes) where I felt that they were needed or of interest. I'm not a historian, and perceptions and memories are fallible, but I've done my best to make it as accurate as possible. That said, I have used a bit of editorial licence here and there, to make it all flow.

So now, enough of *me* blethering, let's start by meeting Rena's parents, over 100 years ago!

Part One
Rena's Story

1

A Splendid Scottish Start to Life

My dad was Thomas Robertson Stewart. My mum *hated* her name: she was Andrewina! Her sisters called her Reenie; she preferred Rena, and that's how I got my name. When I was born, there were arguments about what I should be called. It was fairly obvious that I was going to be the last of that generation. My maiden aunts were all very keen that I should be named after *them*. There was a delay registering the birth certificate, but one day my dad came home from his job at the bank and said: 'Oh, by the way, I've just registered the birth certificate.' So, my mum asked: 'What's her name?' and my dad said: 'Rena, after you!'

My mother's family consisted of nine girls and one boy (you can imagine how spoilt *he* was)! The girls were among those who were, rather unkindly, called 'the two million surplus women', caused by the First World War. Five of them never married. Most of them became schoolteachers, except the youngest, who was very modern and became a shorthand typist. Being a teacher was the ambition of the majority of girls then, I think.

My father always wanted to be a trained musician (a pianist), but he wasn't good enough to earn a living. He had to give up and go into a bank instead, which he didn't like very much. But he found that one of his colleagues played the violin and the other played the cello, so they formed a trio. They used to come to our house to practice. The only piece they ever got up to sufficient standard for playing in public was the *Trio in G* by Haydn, with the *Gypsy Rondo* at the end of it, so my school days were marked by doing my homework in the same room as they were practising the *Gypsy Rondo*.[1] There was only one room heated, as we didn't have enough coal to heat any other rooms.

My mother didn't have a job: *none* of the women did in those days. She was a housewife. [Rena later wrote to me to say that she had remembered that her mother *did* have a job after all and was, in fact, very proud of it. However, she couldn't remember what it was!] There were two of us: me and my sister Isobel, who was christened Isabella. Isobel was nine years older. She once asked my parents: 'Why did you wait so long?' and they said: 'We waited 'til we could afford a second one.'

I was born in a village called Lundin Links, on the shores of the Firth of Forth. I always had great trouble when we had to get our long-distance calls through the operator, explaining that it wasn't anything to do with *London*, it was Lun-din, and it wasn't Lincs as in *Lincolnshire*, it was Links as in golf course [of which the small village boasts two]. So that was the village I was born in.

My first memory – and I don't know how old I was – is I remember my mother wheeling a pram and saying, very crossly: 'A big girl like you ought to be walking.' I was lazy even then!

But I had a happy childhood; a happy home life. There was lots of music, and we had a wireless set. It was the first one in the road, and people came round to listen to it. It was a big box thing, with a battery that had to be recharged at the local garage, and it was so heavy that only my father could take it there. I always remember George V: 'Are you listening, children? This is the King speaking to you' – so I sat up straight![2]

I went to Lundin Mill Public School. Lundin *Links* was a modern thing. There was a mill there which ceased to function, so they decided not to call the place 'mill' if there wasn't a mill there. I was passionate about reading, from about the age of 3, and I loved school. I was always the top!

We never stayed in Lundin Links in the school holidays, though: we always went to Glen Lyon, in Perthshire. We had a cottage there, and we'd spend the whole summer. We had more *friends* in Glen Lyon but a lot of *family* in Lundin Links. Even as a student, I'd head to Glen Lyon in the holidays.

When my mother and father got married, in 1913, there was not a question from my father that their honeymoon would be spent in Glen Lyon. At the time, they had to stay in digs on a farm or something. The story was, on the first day of the honeymoon they took the mail motor [post van] up the glen. You could go *up* with him, but you couldn't arrange to go *back* very easily. So, my father took my mother up the glen to the nearest thing to a village – only a few houses – and then walked down the 10 miles, calling at every house and introducing my mum. And everywhere, they'd get a

---

* Stroupach

I (a non-Scot) wasn't familiar with the word 'stroupach', and Rena wasn't sure how to spell it, so I contacted an organisation called The Scots Language Centre. A representative, Dauvit Horsbroch, kindly explained: 'The word stroupach (pronounced with an "oo") means a (little/quick) cup of tea. It derives from the Scots word "stroup" which means "spout" or "mouth" (of a kettle, or anything from which liquid comes). So, in the sense used here, you might say in English "a quick cup of tea with a light snack".'

'stroupach'– a drink and something to eat.* Dad had nine hard-boiled eggs, and my mum, seven!

My dad did volunteer for the First World War. He was perhaps 32, so too old to be conscripted, but he volunteered. However, he was blind in one eye, and that was enough for him to be rejected. I suppose that was lucky – yes, I might not have been here if he hadn't been rejected!

2

St Andrews: Best Years and Bombs

My sister went to university in Edinburgh. That was in the days when not many women went to university, and she was granted a 'letter' rather than a degree. I was supposed to follow in her footsteps, but my parents thought St Andrews was less likely to be bombed. Ironically, St Andrews *did* get bombed!*

I decided to study languages because I loved poetry, and I thought that if I concentrated on French and German, I'd have access to a whole new world. [Little did Rena know!] I started my degree in 1940, and even then, I already knew that I wanted to work in the news. I think I was fed up with people at that time who thought that if you were an Arts graduate you would become a teacher, and that would be that. One of the people I was friendly with at St Andrews was studying medicine, and as a doctor your fate was laid out for you right from the beginning. That friend greeted me once as 'Miss Rena Stewart, teacher!' I thought, *I'd rather scrub floors than be a teacher*!

St Andrews was a *fabulous* place to study. I remember going and sitting my finals. I came back and Mum asked how they went, and I said: 'I don't know, and I don't care; I've just had three of the happiest years of my life there!' Of course, there was a man involved ... [Rena didn't go into details on her mystery man. I recognised quickly that she was a private person, so I didn't pry, though of course I was itching to know!]

There was a dance every Saturday, and everybody would go. They went whether they danced or not – it was a social gathering. There was Scottish dancing and – how would you call it? – more *modern* dancing. Scottish dancing can vary a great deal, from beautiful footwork to dashing in and having fun. While we were at St Andrews it wasn't *conventional* dancing; it was more about making a lot of noise!

It was strange, studying at university during a war. But we didn't get bombed a *lot* – it was a one-off thing. It was the night that they had the Clydeside bombings – and that was absolutely *flattened*.* The bombs that fell on St Andrews were from the German planes, jettisoning their bombs so they didn't have to carry the weight back home. The bombing didn't affect the centre – more the suburbs – but the university *was* affected.

One of the things we did was that Wednesdays for undergraduates was a day off. You were supposed to take part in games etc., but the university sent out a message; that we should realise that the university was struggling with staffing because of the war. So, we volunteered to help wherever help was needed. After the bombings, we were working in the library. It was *incredible*: the books were all tightly jammed, but if you took one out, a whole lot of glass fell out too. That was because the windows had been blown out and the glass was stuck between the pages!*

> *** Books and bombs**
> Rena's recollection that St Andrews was bombed after the attack/s on Clydeside was not correct. St Andrews was bombed three times during the war: in August and October 1940, and in August 1942. The Clydeside (or Clydebank) Blitz occurred in March 1941.[1] The Luftwaffe conducted two air raids on the town of Clydebank, near Glasgow, which was a centre for shipbuilding and munitions-making. The town was almost entirely destroyed, with over 1,000 people killed and 1,000 more injured. Records state that it was actually the bombing of St Andrews in October *1940* that led to 'hundreds of fragments of glass [having] to be removed from the bindings of library books.'[2]

One of the characters at the university was a man called Professor D'Arcy Thompson. He was larger than life. I had volunteered with my friend Cecil to help in the library (well, Cecil was really Cecilia – Cecil was her nickname). D'Arcy Thompson was a large man with an *enormous* white beard, and he said: 'Who are these two little people, and what do they think they're doing?!'

I had *such* a good time at St Andrews, but I never went back to do the honours [Rena did an 'ordinary' bachelor's degree, without the honours part]: I had discovered there was a big world out there, and I wanted to be *in* it!

3

Signing Up: Silk or Khaki?

My friend Aggie (Agnes Gardner) and I graduated in 1943. We'd met when we were filling up matriculation [enrolment] forms in 1940. She could also have gone on to take an honours degree, but we both thought we'd done enough hanging about, and that we should do something about the war. Our age group was due to be called up later that year, but we decided to get in first, because, being called up, we might have landed in a munitions factory, or anywhere. So, we volunteered for the ATS [the Auxiliary Territorial Service]; in other words, the women's army corps. Actually, we wanted to join the Wrens [the Women's Royal Naval Service]. We were 20 years old, and the choice between wearing black silk stockings and Lisle thread ones and khaki: there was no contest! However, the Wrens were full up at that stage. The only vacancies they had were for mess orderlies, so we were diverted to the ATS.

We were interviewed and waited a *very* long time. As the months went by, we had medicals, tests in German, etc. Nobody told us why it was taking so long to call us up, and nobody told us at first where we were going – until we had signed the Official Secrets Act.[1] We weren't actually called up until November.

4

Basic Training: Ranks and Rifles

We were never *asked* if we wanted to go to Bletchley beforehand; we were just called up in the usual way and sent to a training camp in Guildford, at the end of 1943. We were then told we would be going to Bletchley, which of course didn't mean anything to us at that time: no one knew what *happened* at Bletchley! We were just told that we were being sent to a very secret place – so secret that we would never be able to talk about it – and that if we didn't want to do that, they would find another posting for us. Who could have chosen *that* alternative?![1] [80 years later, in Rena's sitting room in Ealing, I noticed a Bletchley Park postcard pinned to the wall, saying: '*I hereby promise that no word of mine shall betray, however slightly, the great trust placed in me.*']

So, we did a fortnight's basic training in Guildford, learning such useful skills as how to fall in in three ranks, how to salute and so on. We didn't do rifle training. However, at university there was a cadet unit for men, and they decided to form a cadet unit for women, so we were taught to use a rifle *there* – though we were taught with a broomstick! I don't suppose I'd have been much good.

I remember, at the camp in Guildford we had a church parade one day. We were all lined up and the cry went out: 'Church of England: fall out! Roman Catholics: fall out! Nonconformists: fall out!' My friend Aggie and I were left standing there, all on our own, and the sergeant came over, in a furious temper, and said: 'What do you think you're *doing*?!' and we said: 'Well, we're not Nonconformists, we're Church of Scotland!'[2] I can still picture the place where we were left standing.

5
Officially Secret

We were then sent on a course in Hampstead, staying in army conditions in these great big, multimillion-pound houses in Fitzjohn's Avenue that had been requisitioned by the Army. It was only after we signed the Official Secrets Act that we were let into the Enigma secret [that they had broken the code], but only the most basic outline at that stage.[1] We weren't told much detail about it.

It was a very interesting course. The main thing I remember about it is that we learned about German army and navy ranks, their British equivalents and the chain of command – so we knew a bit about that. We also learned about the importance of extreme secrecy. We were told we would be log readers, which sounded the most boring job on Earth, but fortunately, when we got to Bletchley we were all assigned to different departments.[2]*

> *** Log readers, reassigned**
> One of the helpful historians at the Bletchley Park Trust, Dr Thomas Cheetham, noticed the point that Rena made about the girls receiving training at Hampstead and being destined to become boring-old log readers. This, he said, indicates that she and her friends must have been recruited by MI8 (army signals intelligence) and originally intended to serve in a section called 'SIXTA', which it controlled. SIXTA was the main radio traffic analysis section at Bletchley (which involved analysing *patterns* of enemy messages, rather than their content).[3] The higher-ups must then have changed their plans, however, because Rena and co. were reassigned to a department called Hut 3. There, they would serve as a link between the German Book Room (see Chapter 7) and a unit called the Sorting Watch, which was part of SIXTA. Hut 3 didn't employ many ATS women, Dr Cheetham said, and so that made them a bit special!

6

Bletchley Beginnings

On arrival at Bletchley, in about February 1944, my friend Margery Forbes and I were allocated to a unit called 'The German Book Room', along with another Scottish graduate, Elma Morley. I don't know where the others went, except for Aggie: I knew *she* was in the Military Index.* We had been so well briefed on the need for secrecy that we never spoke about work. I stayed in touch with Aggie after the war, though at some point she married – I can't remember her married name [Glynn] – and she went to live in Vancouver.

> * Aggie and the Military Index
> I wasn't sure what 'the Military Index' was; nor was Rena (given the requirement for secrecy that was in place at the time), so I asked the Bletchley Park Trust. The Trust's Oral History Officer, Jonathan Byrne, explained that:
>
> 'The Military Index, sometimes referred to as the Army Index, in Hut 3*, was a card index of significant information from decrypted messages. There would have been cards for types of equipment, individuals, places, and anything else that intelligence analysts might have needed to look up, either for day-to-day intelligence reports or longer-term study. Each entry on the card would have had a brief summary of information and a reference to the source. In modern terms, the indices were databases.'

Incidentally, we joined up as privates and were made lance corporals on arrival at Bletchley, because privates couldn't handle secret documents. We were duly promoted; some of us (including me) to sergeant, and some to CSM (company sergeant major). This was quite arbitrary, as the people dealing with our promotion didn't know what work we were doing.[1]

We three were immediately sent on another course, to learn touch typing. [Rena's typist auntie would have been proud, had she known!] The Army didn't have any courses just for typing, so we had to pretend that we were going to work in company offices. We also learnt shorthand and about army forms. The men wouldn't admit it, but they wouldn't have known how to type; that was considered a *woman's* job. But if they became journalists later on, they jolly well had to learn!

7

The German Book Room

The German Book Room was a great big room, with typewriters all over the place. There were about 40 people – all women – but it was shiftwork, so we were never all there at the same time. The shifts were 8 am to 4 pm and 4 pm to 8 am.*

GBR came under Hut 3. It was separated from Hut 3 by a corridor, and I remember we went up some steps, which puzzles me now. There was a woman in charge: Jane Luxmoore.[1] Everybody said she was the daughter (or wife?) of a high court judge, but she didn't throw her weight about. She was a civilian; they were nearly *all* civilians.

---

* **Hut 3 and the German Book Room**
'Hut 3', under whose remit the German Book Room came, produced military intelligence from the decrypts of Enigma and other sources. This intelligence was code-named 'Ultra'. Decrypts were messages that had been converted back into their original form, readable by humans. See later for a Bletchley Park jargon buster.

Colleagues in Hut 6 deciphered coded German army and air force messages, and these decrypts came to Hut 3 (via a conveyor belt) for translation and analysis. The German Book Room was established in 1940. The role of the women of GBR was to type up transcriptions of the messages, in their original language, and to note down action taken.

Hut 3 was located within an office block, but the exact location of GBR within it has long been a bit of a mystery. I've tried to solve this, by combining evidence from historians with Rena's testimony. For details, see Part Three – Mystery Two.

Rena may have misremembered the shift timings for GBR, since the first shift that she mentioned would have been twice as long as the second. She might have meant 8 am to 4 pm and 4 pm to midnight. In any case, a third shift (a night watch) was added to GBR in February 1945. This brought it into line with most of the rest of Hut 3, and the Park more generally, which operated 24 hours for most of the war.[2]

The three of us were allocated a little side room off the main office: me, Margery and Elma Morley. We were good friends. Elma only died last year – or perhaps early this year. [Elma died in June 2023.] She married a Dutchman. She came over to Britain a lot, and we met up a lot, but we couldn't really keep up a close friendship. She knew she was under a death sentence, as it were, and so she sent emails to people to say goodbye. It choked me up, you know, and I couldn't answer. [I found this terribly sad to hear. However, Elma's daughter, Ellie Wasmoeth, later told me that her mother had actually *phoned* Rena and Aggie (Margery had already died by that time), and so it seems likely that they *did* get to say farewell, after all.]

I should mention that my job entailed neither code-breaking nor translating: the decrypts came in from Hut 3, and I typed them, in German. There was a window through to the big room, where we'd get bundles of secrets. The decrypts were in a form that was not very easy to read. They were strips of paper, stuck onto other strips of paper, which had come straight from the Morse code. They had been broken up into five-letter groups by the time we got them, and the Intelligence Corps people had examined them to see if there was anything very urgent. I felt most of it had happened by the time it came to us – the important ones had gone to Allied commanders *long* before we saw them. We just typed them up into readable typescripts. It sounds like copy-typing but there were lots of mis-hearings. Of course, there were some corrupt groups in the morses that had come through. We were told not to make too-wild guesses about what was missing, but it was usually pretty obvious. That was really why we had to know German properly. It was called 'the German Book Room' because the decrypts were then made into a kind of book form, so that people could read them more easily. The books were useful for people who didn't know the Enigma secret, because there was no immediate evidence of where the information had come from.[3] They were also easier for the Intelligence Corps people working on long-term projects.

'Enigma' was a machine for encoding secret messages [or rather, enciphering and deciphering them – the jargon-buster explains the difference].* Basically, it looked like a typewriter, but in fact it had a QWERTY keyboard where you pressed one key, and what came out was a different letter. I don't know the technical term for it or anything, but the wheels inside this thing operated, and they were changed every day. The Germans thought it was basically an unbreakable code, but Bletchley managed to break it, with the help of machines that were devised by Alan Turing and others.

I didn't see the Enigma machine while I was working at Bletchley, but I *have* seen it since. Some time ago, I had a weekend cottage in a village called Soulbury, about eight miles from Bletchley, and as I didn't want to be the sort of commuter that paid no attention to village life, I joined the Women's Fellowship and the Women's Institute. The Fellowship in the early 1990s had two local ladies come along who were fighting to get Bletchley Park preserved, so I knew, right from the beginning, that it was going to open. After it was opened, to begin with just every second week at the weekend, I used to take people who were visiting me at the cottage to see what was to be seen at that time, which wasn't a great deal. I saw the Enigma machines then.

By the time I started working at Bletchley, Enigma had been broken; code breaking had, I suppose, been a success. However, of course it was not quite as simple as that, because the Germans then – I think they must have had some kind of inkling that things weren't quite as secure as they thought – made the machines more complicated. There was, in fact, a period – I believe in 1942 – when the codes *weren't* broken, so they had to kind of start again from scratch.*

> ** Shark attack!*
> Dr Cheetham (Bletchley Park historian) explained to me that Rena was alluding here to what was called the 'Shark' blackout, in naval Enigma. The Bletchley Park website describes a 'new, more complex Enigma machine for use by … U-boats in the Atlantic'. This development meant that it was no longer possible to read messages that German submarines hunting the vital Atlantic convoys were sending. But never fear, staff at the Park broke the new code by the end of the year![4]

We were never told where our work went after us, and we didn't ask, because we knew we wouldn't be told. Again, I had no idea about Enigma – nor Bombes.* And of course, towards the end of the war there was a programme on television about Enigma, about people working at Bletchley, which wasn't the same as Enigma at all. But it was so laden with guilt and sadness, whereas the main thing about our stay at Bletchley was that we had a great time! I never did discover what the meaning of the programme was, but I think they were trying to make it sound awfully serious and important.[5]

It was very exciting, working at Bletchley, though the actual *work* was quite hard. It varied, of course. Some of the messages were quite dull. You would get ones with lots of figures in them; returns of ammunition and things like that, which were of great interest to the intelligence people, but not of great interest to read. Somebody had written on the messages if they were 'Fish' or 'Tunny', and we also had some Lorenz ones.* I didn't know what the terms meant.

I think the most interesting thing I ever got to type was on the Lorenz code, which was going directly to Hitler. Field Marshal von Kesselring had done a sort of *tour d'horizon* to all the military areas – of what he expected to happen.[6] That was absolutely fascinating! I don't remember what it said, but it was very detailed. I was very excited when I realised how important this message was. I just wished *all* the messages were as interesting as that!

> *** Bletchley Park jargon buster:**
> Many people associate Bletchley Park with Enigma, but Enigma wasn't the only cipher system for messages that staff at the Park worked on – there were dozens, including Lorenz. I've struggled to get to grips with Enigma, Lorenz and the other terms that Rena mentioned. Having done my best to do so, here's a summary:[7]
>
> - **Code (vs cipher)**: First of all, the terms 'code' and 'cipher' are both ways to disguise a message, but they do mean different things. A cipher is essentially an algorithm. Perhaps the most basic one would be A = 1, B = 2, C = 3, etc. (in which case, 'Rena' would be 18-05-14-01). Codes are pre-arranged words, so if 'coffee' meant 3pm and 'Rena' meant Bletchley Park, a message saying 'Coffee today? Love, Rena' could reveal the place and time for a secret rendezvous. The Germans changed their code words daily, making the system very difficult to crack, but the *combination* of codes and ciphers made it even more so.[8] By the way, dear reader, there's an encoded, enciphered message hidden somewhere in this book. I've written it using the methods above. Find it if you can!
> - **Enigma**: The Enigma machine was a device for enciphering and deciphering messages (so, using numbers, not code, though code words were built into the messages). Enigma was used by German industry to begin with, and later by the German military, during the Second World War. The machine was a portable system which resembled a typewriter. It used Morse code and produced short messages only.
> - **Bombe**: A 'Bombe' was an electromechanical device, used by staff at Bletchley Park and its outstations, to help to determine the daily settings of the Enigma machine.
> - **Teleprinter**: A teleprinter was an electromechanical device for sending and receiving typed messages, through various communication channels. These were sent from point-to-point and from one point to multiple points.[9]
> - **'Fish'**: 'Fish' was a generic term for all enciphered teleprinter traffic and its decrypts. The nickname was coined after staff at Bletchley

> Park realised that the Germans called one of their wireless teleprinter transmission systems 'Sägefisch' ('Sawfish'). This was because its aerial array resembled the chainsaw-like tail of a sawfish. Each network in the system (each involving just two specific points) was then given a fishy name, like 'Jelly Fish', 'Octopus' or 'Squid'.[10] Fish ciphers were deciphered in large part with the help of Colossus, the world's first, large-scale electronic digital computer.[11]
>
> - **Lorenz**: Lorenz was the name of a German company which produced one of the other cipher systems that staff at Bletchley worked on (along with Enigma). Lorenz machines were used only by Hitler, his high command and top generals, so breaking into them was like being 'a fly on the wall of Hitler's bunker'.[12] The machines were ciphers that could be attached to a standard teleprinter. They enciphered and deciphered messages only, rather than sending and receiving them. Lorenz networks were simpler than Enigma ones, involving point-to-point links only. However, the machines were more advanced, faster and more secure than Enigma. They could also encipher/decipher longer, more detailed messages (as Rena mentioned), and do so automatically.
> - Finally, **'Tunny'**: 'Tunny' (or tuna) was the first fishy cover name that staff at Bletchley came up with, when they identified the first Lorenz link. The staff developed 'tunny machines' to allow them to print out deciphered messages from the Lorenz, in German. Eventually, the term was used much more broadly, and the link was renamed 'Codfish'.
>
> And now, back to Rena, toiling away in Hut 3.

It was quite taxing work at Bletchley Park, because we worked six days on and one day off.* Of course we had crises, when everybody was working around the clock, and it was stressful and so on. When, later on, there was a tremendous increase in work volume – possibly around D-Day – we worked night shifts as well. But in the Park, the mood was quite free and easy, actually. You chose your days on a big chart, which was put up every month. You could have a weekend off by having the Saturday of one week and the Sunday of the next, but that really wasn't a very good idea, because then you had a long period before another day off. I didn't get *home* on leave, as a 48-hour pass was no use to get up to Scotland.

> *** GBR jobs: not for the faint-hearted**
> As Rena said, the job of a GBR woman was taxing. The author John Jackson wrote a book on Hut 3. In it, he described the kind of person required for GBR. They (well, she) had to:
>
> - ✓ 'possess a sense of individual responsibility' (because the pressure the organisation was under didn't allow for much contact with bosses)
> - ✓ have 'very good German, acquired either at university or abroad'
> - ✓ be of 'an ideal age of 20–30'
> - ✓ have 'good typing' and
> - ✓ have '[good] eyesight,' as 'the strain of specialised typing for long hours proved too much for older people.'
>
> This, he added, was not work for the 'excitable and highly sensitive type'![13]
>
> In the book's foreword, Peter Calvocoressi, who was head of the Air Section in Hut 3, paid respect to Hut 3's 'backroom boys and girls,' who 'seldom gather many laurels'. He emphasised that the 'sprinkling of [mostly female] high-grade minions' contributed greatly to the success of this 'illustrious molehill'.[14]
>
> Work in the molehill really got intense in about February 1945 (not necessarily just around D-Day, as Rena suggested). According to Dr Cheetham, this was due to a change in German callsign procedure, when German signals officers were permitted to make up callsigns at random. This change made it much harder for Hut 6 to identify which networks messages were sent on. One consequence was that GBR took on 'a much more active role in the intelligence production process'. Previously, they had been 'the last link in the chain'; now they were involved earlier and more fully. Cheetham added that Rena's memory of strips of paper stuck on to others indicates that these hadn't yet been processed. All decrypts now had to be 'emended' (corrected/revised and made more readable), rather than just some of them, and they all had to be typed in the books. This, he explained, helped to give the codebreakers and traffic analysts in Hut 6 and SIXTA as much information as possible.

We did sense at the time how important Bletchley was to Britain winning the war. We knew that we were reading German messages more or less at the same time as the Germans were, and that the people in the field relied on Bletchley completely. It was drummed into us that if we spilled the beans in any way, we were endangering people's lives, and also the outcome of the war. For instance, we were told that if anybody tried to guess what we were doing, we weren't to say: 'No, it's not that,' because by process of elimination you could get to the secret. We could also only go to our *own* offices; we couldn't go to people in *other* offices, and we just went home after we'd finished our shift. Nor did we see any of the VIP visitors who came to Bletchley.

8

Park Life

The Park itself – the main building there – we called it 'the mansion'. It was an Edwardian-style building and had been built by a financier [Sir Herbert Leon] who wanted to include every possible style of architecture into it. It was a perfect mess! But where *we* worked – we were in *huts*. It was quite a big estate and had huts all over the place. In fact, I never set foot into the mansion in all the time I was there. We just walked to our hut and back again and never went anywhere near it.

When you went into the Park, you forgot about being in the Army. On the whole, Bletchley Park never took account of ranks; they were just ignored. Nobody bothered to salute. It was difficult, though, because you *did* have to remember to salute senior officers. You'd have a corporal giving orders to a major, and things like that, and that happened all over the place in Bletchley.*
In fact, we – my friends and I – never got any further than sergeant, and there were WAAF [Women's Auxiliary Air Force] officers who were junior to us. It wasn't all army or air force people though, by any means: in fact, most of the women were in the *naval* service.[1] There were a lot of civilians, too.

---

* **Going Bush in Bletchley**
During the war, one of Rena's friends from Bletchley, Michael Pocock, wrote an amusing article about the lack of military discipline in the Park. He called it '*Going Bush in Bletchley*'. Many years later, Rena donated the article to the museum.[2] She told them that Pocock had served on the frontline but been transferred to Bletchley for health reasons.

In the article, Michael casts himself as a budding anthropologist, sent by the British Museum to study the 'strange tribe' of Bletchley Park. He describes the tribe's 'long low huts similar to hen-coops' and remarks on the inhabitants' lack of hygiene, comparing it to 'the less disciplined units of the Italian militia'. The women, he writes, are 'strictly segregated' from the men. They dress in 'drab uniforms' but are occasionally to be seen in sports kit, consisting of 'anything from a brassiere and running shorts to a full-length evening gown'. He witnesses 'the simple people' 'hurry to their

> appointed tasks with the zeal and enthusiasm of the habitually unpunctual' and pray to their god, 'The Next Meal'. He reports: 'I could discern among the knots of chattering, laughing tribesmen the failing memory of three ranks,' and that 'all military murmurs will be hushed in the tender tranquillity of Shangri-la'. He concludes: 'It is a strange and sad thought that one day peace will break out and B.P., which has sheltered so many for so long, will be but a fragrant memory.'

We lived in Shenley Road Military Camp, adjoining the Park.³ Camp life was *awful* – very spartan. Firstly, the people in charge of our day-to-day life there didn't know what we were *doing* at Bletchley Park. We had a woman commanding officer – Senior Commander Kemp – who demanded to be shown what we were doing. They did eventually take her into the Park. I don't know what they showed her, but it wasn't the full story!

Kemp was determined that her ATS unit would be 'proper'. We were living a kind of double life: working hard when we were in the Park, and also being expected to do compulsory PE [physical education], route marches, cross-country runs and cleaning out the barracks. We always had to put up with *that*! The cross-country runs always left by the back gate of the camp and came back round the front gate. If you loitered a bit, you could let them all go out the back gate and then nip off to the NAAFI [Navy, Army and Air Force Institute] for a coffee, and sneak down to the front gate.⁴ That was the kind of thing that happened with Commander *Kemp* in charge. At this distance in time, I can actually feel sorry for her!

One example of her discipline was that the road up to the camp was a dark lane, with trees and bushes either side. So, when people were coming home from dates, it was the ideal place to have a 'prolonged good night'. When Senior Commander Kemp came to hear about this, she thought: *We can't have this – people enjoying themselves!* So, she arranged that the guardroom should send out a patrol every night to break up the clinches. This was christened the Purity Patrol ('P' Patrol for short). There was a poem written about it, called *Mein Kemp*! [The poem – a play on the title of Hitler's autobiography/manifesto, *Mein Kampf* – is believed to have been performed for the last wartime Christmas concert at Bletchley, in 1944.⁵ Rena read the poem at a public event in later life. With a twinkle in her eye, she started:]

> *The ATS are in my charge,*
> *Their urges I control*
> *I never let them roam at large*
> *Without my 'P' Patrol* [etc. etc.]

MEIN KEMP

VERSE:

The ATS are in my charge,
Their urges I control
I never let them roam at large
Without my "P" Patrol.

CHORUS

I keep 'em in as much as poss,
On drill, P.T and paint,
I make 'em understand I'm boss,
I'm Kemp their chief complaint.

VERSE:

My reason is quite plain to see,
I'm out for better mothers,
The standard is laid down by me,
Their own ideas it smothers.

CHORUS.

....

I'm Kemp by night, I'm Kemp by day,
I'm Kemp from first to last,
My girlies must not ever play,
They shall not have a past.

CHORUS

........l..................

And some there are who say I'm sweet,
But others say I ain't,
Abd hold their noses when I pass
And look, and feel quite faint.

CHORUS

......L..................

The silly children say they think
Nine hours are quite enough
But let me tell those idle girls
I'm going to treat them rough.

CHORUS

....

Until the war for freedom's won
Their freedom will get littler
For in this camp I'll have you know
I'm not KEMP but HITLER.

CHORUS

....

I do not shout, I do not bawl,
My stern commands, peremt,
Cry: but happy girls when all
Again can be unkempt.

LAST CHORUS

One thing we learn, one thing observe,
That in life's steady tremp
Whatever we do, will ne'er deserve
A fate that's worse than KEMP.

Mein Kemp - a humorous protest poem about Rena's disciplinarian commanding officer, Senior Commander Kemp. (*Courtesy of the Bletchley Park Trust*)

As for our accommodation, there were 30 of us in a very basic, under-furnished Nissen hut; just army beds and two pegs, and a barrack box for our possessions.⁶ We ate our meals in the Sergeants' Mess in camp and only went into the mess in Bletchley when we were on night shift. The food was *ghastly*. But there were all sorts of things we could do for fun, and we were glad of some recreation when the day was over, or the night! For example, you could go to the cinema – and the motive for that was that it was *warm*. We woke up one morning with ice on the insides of the windows! The huts were heated by coke-burning stoves, which gave off absolutely *toxic* fumes, so you could choose between being suffocated or being frozen to death. The ablutions, for one thing, were in a separate building, so in the middle of the night, if you had to get up, you went out in your dressing gown and slippers. Working with civilians, there was a little bit of resentment there!

However, it wasn't *all* bad. We did have a wind-up gramophone in our hut, and we bought records. The very favourite one was Charles Trenet, *La Mer*.⁷ People would wait for it to come to the end, then lift the needle up and put it back at the beginning. That song brings back memories of Bletchley! [Please do look this song up and listen to it immediately – it's a beauty!]

We had quite a lot of social activity within the Park itself. We had ballroom dances, Scottish dancing and a very good amateur dramatics society, which put on the most *terrific* revues, in a hall in Bletchley.⁸ These were great fun. I can remember hearing a song to the music of *Trees* in a revue.*

*****Trees, please!**
Trees is a poem by an American poet, Joyce Kilmer, written in 1913. Starting: 'I think that I shall never see ... a poem lovely as a tree', Kilmer reflects on the beauty of nature, and on the inability of man to recreate it. The poem was set to music several times, with one version becoming very popular in the Second World War. It was sung (albeit not together) by Nelson Eddy, Robert Merrill and Paul Robeson. These were all interesting characters themselves, including a movie actor and a spy.⁹ Please do look this song up, too!

Anyway, music-and-mischief-minded staff at Bletchley Park created a spoof version of this song, called *Bumph Palace*. 'Bumph' was a rude reference to toilet paper (a metaphor for the reams of paperwork/bureaucracy at Bletchley), and the song is a humorous take on the strange world of the Park. It was performed during a Victory in Japan party, and probably beforehand as well. It's likely that *this* is the revue that Rena remembered, with a smile. The war was ending, and *Bumph Palace* was effectively a souvenir of the

> strange and intense, but also brilliant, time that the staff at Bletchley had experienced there.[10] It started:
>
> *I think that I shall never see*
> *A sight so curious as BP*
> *This place, called up at war's behest*
> *And peopled with the queerly-dressed [etc.]*

In the German Book Room we had a song, to the tune of *My Bonnie Lies Over the Ocean*. I don't remember all the words, but it went something like this [Rena and I had fun singing this together in her sitting room – it was an unforgettable moment:]

> *The days of our hardship are ending,*
> *The war ... la la la la la laaaa,*
> *Our section is forty in number,*
> *We've maidens both short and tall.*
> *Typing, typing, oh for the end of the war, the war,*
> *Typing, typing, we don't want to type any more!*
> *They come from all corners of Britain,*
> *In GBR's net they were caught,*
> *But now that the war's nearly over,*
> *We'll wait with new hope for the dawn.*
> *Typing, typing, oh for the end of the war, the war,*
> *Typing, typing, we **don't** want to type any more!*

[I contacted the Bletchley Park Trust to see if they were aware of this musical masterpiece. They informed me that Rena had actually donated a printed copy of the song – *The Swan Song of G.B.R.* The copy had been signed by the women that worked there, including Rena, Elma and Margery. It's dated 17 May 1945, shortly after VE (Victory in Europe) Day. At that time, spirits at Bletchley would have been high and workloads reduced, even though the war wasn't yet over. Given that so many years had passed, and that Rena was starting to lose her memory, I think she did very well to remember as much of the song as she did! Back to Sergeant Stewart, then, warming up at the Bletchley Park tennis courts.]

We also played tennis – there were courts in the Park. In fact, the story is: when Churchill came, he saw the tennis courts, which were in disrepair, and he

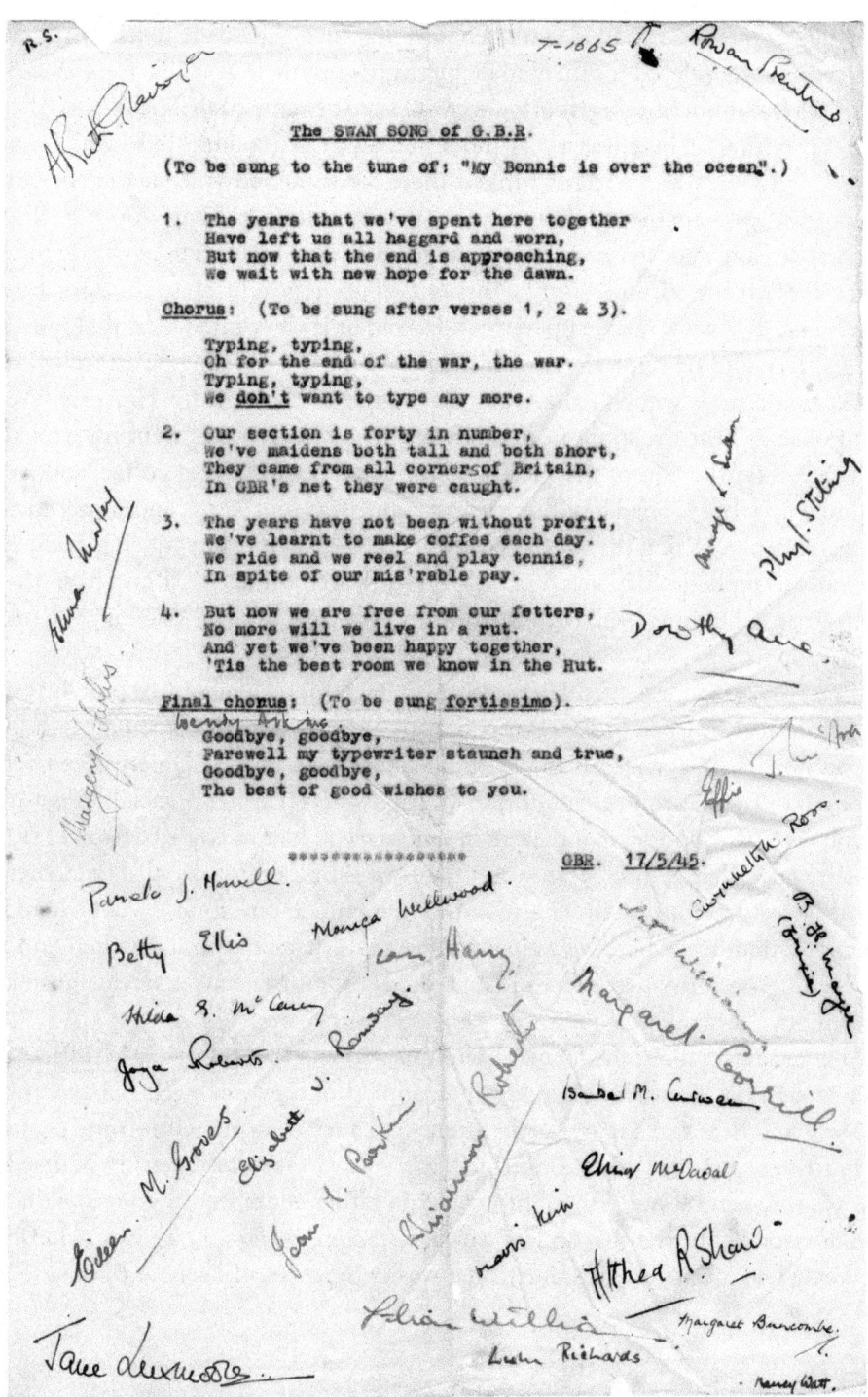

The Swan Song of G.B.R., signed by some of the women who worked there. (*Courtesy of the Bletchley Park Trust*)

thought it would be a good idea for people doing such a good job to have time to play tennis. He ordered for them to be put right and made available for playing!

I did a lot of hitchhiking, too: we were all aged around 20 to 21 and had 21st birthday outings. There was a very modern roadhouse [country pub] which we occasionally went to.[11] We hitchhiked there for somebody's 21st, and the lift we got was in a coal lorry! The driver was very intrigued by us going to this roadhouse: you went in one way and out another, and we tried to persuade him to let us off at the entrance, but he insisted on driving right up to the door. On one occasion, a waiter came up to us and asked us if we wanted a drink. I asked for a sherry, and he said: 'It's two shillings and sixpence – can you afford it?'

We sometimes went to the Corn Exchange in Bedford for concerts. We went once to hear the soprano, Elsie Suddaby, and afterwards went for a meal in a café.[12] At the end of the meal, we wondered about having coffee, and we counted up what we had left. Sometimes coffee was fourpence, and sometimes it was sixpence. When the waitress came back, we asked: 'How much is coffee?' When she replied: 'Sixpence,' we said: 'We won't bother; we'll just have the bill, please.' She came back with the bill and two cups of coffee, saying: 'Go on, have your coffee.'

The other thing was that there was a train to London at about 10 past 4. The morning shift finished at 4, and if you really *belted* it down, you could catch it! If you went *after* 4, you had to pay more. There was an RAF gate where they checked our passes, and if you forgot your pass you had to go back and get it. If you went to London, to a theatre or cinema, you had to come back at 11:30, which was rather awful, because the train would be full of drunks. And then you'd have to be up for the 8 am shift. I remember, one time I went up and went to a matinée, where we were standing at the back of the stalls, then on to an evening performance afterwards. I would sometimes stay at service hostels overnight, if I had a pass to do so.

[I asked Rena about the men at Bletchley, and whether they were gentlemen! She said:] Well, there was the odd rotten apple, but they were well-behaved, on the whole. There *was* a man … [that Rena had a relationship with – once again, I didn't dig, though I'd have loved to]. He was very keen on getting married, but I was too ambitious. I thought I could do rather better in the *newsroom* than as a housewife. In the '40s and '50s it was *dreadful* being a housewife. Hardly anybody had a washing machine. That wasn't for me, so I broke it off.

9

Keeping the Secret

I don't think I'm all that proud of the job I did at Bletchley, but I'm proud of having kept the *secret*, shall we say? Well, you know, it was quite a feat to be able to keep quiet about it, and not be tempted to waft your self-importance and say what you were doing. I didn't tell my *parents* what I was doing. I don't think they wondered very much, to be quite honest, because people didn't. You told them you were doing secret work and that was it: they didn't expect you to say any more. I didn't tell my *friends* anything, either. If they tried to ask, or wondered what you were doing, you changed the subject.

I think the first time I mentioned to others that I had worked at Bletchley must have been in the 1970s, when Colonel Winterbotham's book *The Ultra Secret* was first published.[1] So, I kept it secret for 30 years! And in fact, we were *horrified* when they started writing books about it; we couldn't get over it! How *dare* they?! We had been told we would never be able to tell in our lifetime, and we had *nightmares* about the secret getting out. My particular nightmare was, I was sitting in a railway carriage and suddenly started telling everybody about the Enigma code being broken. I bought the book by Winterbotham, and it was quite unreadable!* I looked up the index later to see what he'd said about Alan Turing, and Turing's name wasn't *in* the index.

Keeping the secret certainly is remarkable in terms of how people see things nowadays. They must think we were very incurious about things, because you didn't ask what other people were doing; you just accepted that it wasn't known. It's quite a relief, you know, to be able to talk about it, and to realise that people *know* about it. It just makes you feel quite proud!

*** Winterbotham – quite unreadable!**
Group Captain Frederick Winterbotham was a Royal Air Force officer. Between 1939 and 1940, he set up the section that would become Hut 3, between 1939 and 1940. He then moved up through the ranks of the Secret Intelligence Service. Rena didn't explain why she thought Winterbotham's book was 'unreadable', so I asked Dr Cheetham. He told me:

> 'Winterbotham's book has attracted quite a lot of criticism. Mostly this is due to his contention that Coventry was 'sacrificed' [to the German bombers] to protect the secret of Ultra [that is, Bletchley Park]. This was a myth which was dismissed very quickly but still rears its head all too often.[2] That may have been Rena's main complaint. Otherwise, Winterbotham knew next to nothing about the processes in Hut 6, or Hut 3 after the very early period after he set it up, so his descriptions of these are full of falsehoods. I do not quite agree with those who would say that Winterbotham should be written off completely, however, as he was still an important figure, whose recollections are unique and useful.'

10

Demob Deferred

When the war ended, of course the *civilian* employees all left Bletchley and were able to look for peace-time work. *We* had another 18 months to put in before we could be demobbed [meaning demobilised; released from the Army].[1] Well, our demob was determined by our age and length of service, and of course none of us were very old nor had been in the Services very long. We were all sent to attend a WOSB (War Officer Selection Board), to be assessed for promotion to officer rank, and we all failed. Bletchley Park had *ruined* us for ordinary army life! They were left with a whole lot of ATS girls who knew German – so what did they do with us? Send some of us to Germany, to join a CSDIC unit (the Combined Services Detailed Interrogation Centre), working for the British Army Intelligence Corps. [Rena would be part of the newly-formed British Army of the Rhine (BAOR)]. This was my first time outside the UK, because being from Scotland we had a long way to go before we even got to the Continent!

11

The Epic Journey to Germany

[This section of the story combines a conversation that I had with Rena with a humorous-yet-serious diary that she wrote about her journey to Germany in September 1945. She called the diary '*FOUR DAYS IN FOUR COUNTRIES – Being an account of the hardships, toils and travails, of a modern Amazon on a trip across battle-scarred Europe.*' Rena's proud nephew, Stewart Maclennan, describes *Four Days* as 'a very early confirmation of her journalistic leanings'.]

On Friday, 31 August 1945, we rose at 5:30 am and toted our 'not wanted on voyage' kitbags to the parade ground before breakfast. After breakfast we paraded, carrying water bottles, haversacks, respirators and tin hats (the reason for these last two items is only known to God and the Army Council), kitbags and greatcoats. We were loaded into trucks and carted like cattle to Temple Meads Station [in Bristol – I presume that they'd been doing some training near there]. There we were lined up, and the RSM [Regimental Sergeant Major], a frightful barmy female, gave the command "Oist kit!' and 'Quick march!' (we could hardly stagger). As the train drew out, she added insult to injury, by saying: 'All the best, girls,' for which she received cat-calls!

We recovered from heaving the kit into the train; then the torture was repeated at Paddington. We had a nice run through Hyde Park and along the Embankment to Fenchurch St. Station (terrific job getting baggage up a flight of stairs), an interval for a meal at Lyons, and then went on to Tilbury Docks.[1] [I presume that PE-avoider Rena was kidding about the run from Paddington Station to Fenchurch St. Station being 'nice', given that it was a distance of about 4½ miles, with heavy bags!]

The first excitement was exchanging money and getting 271 marks (£6.15.6) [six pounds, 15 shillings and sixpence, an equivalent of roughly £339.21 in 2025]. We looked enviously at some NAAFI girls carrying one small haversack. We boarded ship – the '*Ulster Monarch*' – and were thirteen in a small cabin: three-tier berths and three on the floor.[2] There was confusion in the loudspeaker instructions, since the loudspeaker served both the announcements to those on board, and the BBC *Light Programme* [the predecessor of Radio 1 and 2]. After supper (fried egg) we went out on deck to watch the goings-on and had a singsong to the inevitable mouth-organ. There was consternation when the pukka voice on the loudspeaker announced that breakfast would be at 'ow faive threy oh ahs' [05:30 hours].

My burning question was would I be seasick! I spent a somewhat uneasy night, due to swell on the sea. I wasn't sick, though I was wakened at 1 am to be given a paper bag to be sick in if necessary (revolting thought). I rose in time to see the dawn, and there was land in sight when we got up. The only flaw was that there were kippers for breakfast. I got my respirator etc. onto aching shoulders, lifted my kitbag with a swollen hand, and we piled into a truck.

We were first taken to a transit camp, at Hotel Leopold in Ostend. That was not too bad; just the early start and having a lot of luggage to cart about, but that was very routine. Food in the unit was pretty awful – we had bully beef [corned beef] for every meal and dehydrated potatoes like gluey whitewash. However, the hotel was pretty nice: two to a room and running water in rooms. We were kept in during the morning and told not to speak to civilians on the street below, as they would ask for cigarettes, and in no time, we'd have a riot outside! In the afternoon, Margery and I went out to change her marks. After a long and thirsty walk, in fruitless search of the Field Cashier, we went in despair to the NAAFI, hoping *they* would do it. They wouldn't, but two RAMC [Royal Army Medical Corps] corporals, seeing our plight, bought us a drink. At night we were more successful and got 100 francs each.

We had a couple of days in Ostend, and we had a *lovely* time. Margery and I hired bathing costumes, at 10 francs each, and went bathing. There were *lovely* big breakers! Everything in Belgium seemed to be much more luxurious than we were accustomed to in Britain. The town, although bombed a bit and rather shabby as to the paintwork, looked very prosperous and gay. The shops were full of luxuries, and although things were dear, prices could hardly be classed as 'black market'. The exchange rate was 176 francs to a pound. Bread was 4 francs 10, shoes from 200–400 francs, lipsticks 50 francs, peaches 12 francs 1, ices 5 and 1, etc. In the afternoon, we went and squandered over 100 francs on souvenirs, peaches, ices, and a tram trip!

The people in Ostend were fairly well dressed; the women tending to flashiness. Fashions ran to fantastically high wedge-heel shoes and sandals, high hats, short skirts and long jackets (like after the last war) and earrings of peculiar shapes, about the size of small asters. The children had, it seemed, mostly been refugees in England: many of them addressed you in perfect Cockney or broad Scots! When we heard, at about 5 o'clock, that we were to be going the next morning, we thought *too bad*, as we had planned to change more marks and buy lots of things, including a Flemish dictionary. Flemish *fascinates* us. Everyone had a really good time – we were all sorry to leave.

32 The Story of Rena Stewart

For the actual journey to Germany, reveille [the signal to wake up] was sounded at 4:30 am and we left in trucks at 6. We didn't have to carry kitbags; they were taken separately. In fact, we hadn't carried them since we landed. The attitude here was quite different: we were *women* now, not ATS. We got on a very long, very decrepit-looking train with a rather passé engine, which kept stopping and starting, but it was very comfortable. We travelled in first class, so no wooden seats as the men had. Our last glimpse of Ostend was very pleasant: the sun coming up behind the sails of the fishing boats in the harbour.

We travelled through Belgium first of all. The houses were peculiar: long thin ones, about three storeys high and one-room thick, and tiled houses. The country was very flat and marshy.

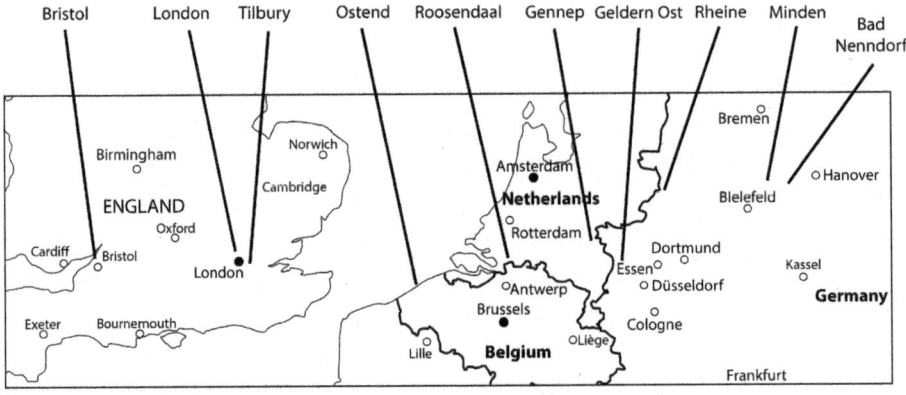

Figure 1: Rena's 600-plus-mile journey to Bad Nenndorf, Germany.

We crossed the Dutch border at Roosendaal. The Dutch were obviously much worse off than the Belgians had been. There were rows of children standing at the side of the railway line, the little girls holding out their aprons, waiting for us to throw out biscuits and sweets from the windows. We had already been advised to take things like that with us because there wasn't going to be much food available on the journey. Everyone gave them as much as they could. At the stations, the adults were on the platform, with apples, pears and tomatoes, and you threw them a cigarette and grabbed an apple or something in return as the train went past. They were pathetically grateful for the cigarettes. At Gennep, we all got out and were taken in trucks to a nearby camp for a meal at about 2:30 pm, and we tried out our *Plattdeutsch* on a railway worker or two![3]

After that, we crossed the German border without realising it – until we saw the camps of German prisoners, all under canvas and surrounded by barbed wire. Some fool threw one of them a sandwich, and instead of picking it up, he positively *snarled* at us. Later, at Geldern Ost, there were some kids by the line – mostly lovely little girls with blonde pigtails, and people felt so sorry for them that the flinging-out of chocolate began again. However, an order was passed round that no more was to be flung out. At that time, we were passing through an area of the German countryside that had been fought over and was very badly devastated by shellfire – I think it would have been about the most bitterly contested part of the British sector just before the Rhine. There was hardly a building standing; hardly an intact roof for miles and miles, and people were living in the road, or in the ruins if they had any roofs at all, though they all looked as if they would fall down any minute. It was most depressing, and you couldn't help feeling sorry for the people.

We reached the Rhine at sunset (the train, with its decrepit engine, had been going very slowly and stopping often). We crossed the Rhine at Rheine, by the famous 'shoogly' bridge*, which we had heard of in Ostend. The bridge was a temporary erection of wooden pillars and iron girders, and the railway line had had to be diverted over it, as all the other bridges around had been totally wrecked. I couldn't say how long it was to get over, but it was very slow. The bridge was shaking all the time, and of course the train overlapped it. We looked right down into the river from the carriage windows, which added to our feeling of insecurity. We were thankful to get across!

> * **'Shoogly'**
> I wasn't familiar with the word 'shoogly' – though I liked it straight away! I guessed that it might be American, but in fact it's Scots for shaky – originally from the Middle English 'shoggle'. It can describe an unsteady object, a disturbed mental state, or be used as a verb to ask someone to shift along on a seat. The phrase 'You're on a shoogly peg' means you're on your last warning. The bridge that Rena and co. crossed on their decrepit train was shaky *and* quite possibly on its last warning![4]

After that, it got dark, and, as there were no lights in the train, there was nothing else to do but go to sleep. And as far as *we* were concerned, of course we had breakfast before 6, a meal about 2:30 pm, and we didn't see anything else until breakfast the following morning. The whole journey took 24 hours, and I think it could be done nowadays in 3 or 4 hours. At 4 am we alighted (or, as the Army will have it, 'detrained', whatever that means) at Minden and were given a hot meal of fish and chips [a strange choice for breakfast, but no doubt welcome]! We finished the journey and arrived at our destination at 6 am.

12

Bad Nenndorf: Back to Work

We ended up in a place called Bad Nenndorf, which is near Hanover.* It's a spa town, and that was the interrogation camp. Where the *prisoners* were was the place where the baths and accommodation for the patients were in the days when it was a spa, and the whole camp was surrounded by 8-foot fences with barbed wire.

> *** Bad Nenndorf**
> The camp at Bad Nenndorf was officially named No. 74 Combined Services Detailed Interrogation Centre, or No. 74 DIC. Its initial purpose was to gather information on the German intelligence services. This was partly to prevent a Nazi revival after the war, which in 1945 was a worrying possibility. It was later used during the Cold War, to help the West to understand the threat from the Soviet Union.[1]

Again, we were assigned to different departments, and I don't know much about what happened to the rest, but my friend Margery Forbes and I were sent to an office under Major Bill Oughton. We were given the task of translating the hand-written statements of prisoners who had been interrogated by another member of the section. Our unit consisted of us two, doing the translations, and a male NCO [non-commissioned officer], who did the interrogations.

[I got in touch with Margery's son, Ed Tarwinski, to let him know that I was writing Rena's story, and to ask him about his mum. Ed sent me a letter that Margery had written to a Bletchley Park friend, Agnes MacMorland (married name Chappell) in September 1945.[2] This was just after she, Rena and the others arrived at Bad Nenndorf. It says: 'Rena and I are working in a lovely big office with two large windows looking out on to the garden,' but that (with faux alarm) 'there is a great danger of our being transferred to the general typing pool ... a huge room where 20 ATS type all day long and are mere stooges'. She wrote that 'The work – mainly translating – is very interesting and promises to be more so,' and that 'we work from 0845 'til 1700 hours, in theory.']

The prisoners were mainly Abwehr people – you know, the German intelligence service people. [Other prisoners included 'SS [Schutzstaffel] criminals who had worked in the concentration camps [and] former managerial staff from large German companies.'][3] And we were quite amused, in a way, to discover that though the German reputation is of efficiency, they really spent more time infighting with the other intelligence outfits than they did on winning the war, I suppose.

When we first went out there, well, we didn't know what to expect. And neither did the authorities: they didn't know if there was going to be any kind of uprising. We were only allowed to go out in daylight, in pairs, and with a soldier with us. It wasn't until they realised there wasn't going to be any kind of rebellion or anything that we were able to move about more freely and lead a more normal life.

[In her letter, Margery went on to say of the security situation: 'The escort business may seem rather extravagant to you, but believe me, it's really necessary to be armed here. I think that for the men it isn't so bad, but the women would really be in grave danger, even if they went about in twos and threes, after dusk. You should see the way people look at us! The German women especially either look pointedly away from us as we pass, or look as if they could cheerfully scratch our eyes out. It is unfortunate that, all through the war, the place has been used as a hospital and convalescent home, as it is very suitable, being composed mainly of nursing-homes, hotels and boarding houses; it means that all the German soldiers about are minus arms and legs and look very ill, while the conquerors stride about hale and hearty. It's illogical, but the contrast is there. Anyway, I don't think you need feel envious of our lot. I think that Bletchley and Nenndorf just about balance in good and bad points.']

[Rena talked about her male colleagues:] Now, the people who were doing the questioning were all men, and they were *all* – I think without exception – German Jewish refugees, who had been in the Pioneer Corps, and whose native language was German. [The Royal Pioneer Corps was a British Army light engineering corps which, at the beginning of the war was 'the only British military unit in which enemy aliens could serve'.[4]] They would carry out interrogations, prisoners were asked to submit written statements, and we got the written statements.

Officially, we weren't supposed to go into the camp where the prisoners were at *all*, but I went there a couple of times. Well, there was one time when the NCO in our unit was interrogating in our section. One of the people who he was questioning was a Belgian who had definitely spied for the Nazis. He claimed to have been a double agent and spied for the British as well. Sean, the NCO, didn't think he was lying but thought he was a fantasist; just making himself important. He put in a request to the authorities that the man should be released. But the colonel in charge, Colonel Stephens*, said no; they were returning him to Belgium to stand trial, and he was going to be convicted of being a Nazi spy. The day that Sean had to go and tell him this, he asked me to come with him to break the news, because he thought he might burst into tears, and that my presence might, in some way, inhibit that. But it didn't; he *did* burst into tears. I think that would have been a death sentence for the man, but I never heard what actually happened to him in the end.

There was a case – it was after I left – when there was a court of inquiry into the treatment of the prisoners at the camp. It was a small minority of the soldiers who were responsible. I felt furious! It was horrible. But you know, there *was* some discipline applied. I can't remember what.* But I must have been a bit unlucky with camp commanders. Colonel Stephens had been in charge of the CSDIC camp in the UK, Camp 020, which was concerned with interrogating German spies who'd been caught. He cropped up in a book by Ben Macintyre called *Double Cross*, which is about double agents. He is described in the book as being known as 'Tin Eye', 'on account of the monocle permanently screwed into his right eye'. He's described as 'xenophobic, rude, manipulative, ruthless and brilliant', and as having subjected spies to 'intense interrogation using every method to extract the truth short of physical violence'.[5] Well actually, that last proviso didn't hold good in Germany, because there were some of the warders who *were* beating up the prisoners. And the prisoners were mostly people who were being interrogated to find out how much they sympathised with the Nazis. I think they'd all been members of the Nazi party, but most of them pleaded that they *had* to join, otherwise they would have never got promotion. So that was Colonel Stephens, who we had to put up with after having endured Senior Commander Kemp!

> *** Colonel 'Tin Eye' Stephens, and bad stuff at Bad Nenndorf**
> I wanted to find out a bit about 'Tin Eye' Stephens, so I asked a friend of mine in the Intelligence Corps. She put me in touch with Nick Fox, a former Int. Corps colonel who is knows a lot about the history of the organisation. Colonel Fox provided the following information on Colonel Stephens:
>
> > 'Lt Col Robin 'Tin Eye' Stephens, Indian Army, was seconded to MI5 in 1939. He had, previously to Bad Nenndorf, commanded Camp 020, a detention centre in Surrey dealing with German spies. He was a 'formidable, forceful and energetic character who had an extraordinary ability to break even the hardest of spies', using 'every kind of mental

> pressure' to 'break' prisoners' – but not physical measures.'[6] This description tallies with Rena's account – but there was more:

The situation in the camp at Bad Nenndorf was much worse than Rena realised. Colonel Fox told me that, in 2005, *The Guardian* newspaper submitted a Freedom of Information request to the Foreign Office, which reported widespread abuse and neglect.[7] However, Rena was neither involved in nor aware of this at the time, and Colonel Fox stated that the *Guardian* article 'seems a little skewed'. He said that some people *were* found guilty of various offences, and that Colonel Stephens did go on trial for alleged torture, but that he was acquitted.

13

A Top-secret Task

In January 1946, after we had been at Bad Nenndorf for several weeks [months, in fact!], Major Oughton came into our office one day, looking very solemn. He said to Margery and me: 'I want you to stop doing whatever you are doing and work together on translating this document. Take as long as you like, but there must be no mistakes: make sure it's *absolutely perfect*. You must agree on all the details, and you're not to tell anyone about it.' He didn't say what the document was, and he left without giving any further information, but it turned out to be Hitler's will.*

The document didn't say: 'I, Adolf Hitler, give my last will and testament', or something like that, because then I think we would have known right away. I think the *original* may have had 'I Adolf Hitler', but it wasn't on the document *we* had. However, it was as we went through it that we realised that it was Hitler's will. It was pretty obvious from the contents, and we were pretty sure it couldn't have been anything else. And when we *did* realise what it was, we were amazed, and awe-struck at being entrusted with it. It meant there was all the more onus on us to get the translation absolutely right!

There were actually two wills – a political one and a personal one. I should emphasise that they were not *legal* documents, but simply saying what Hitler wanted to happen after his death. One was about what he wanted to happen in the *political* field, the other – which was much shorter – was what he wanted to happen to his *family*. That was the one we were to translate. We didn't translate the political will. I don't know why. Of course, we were so imbued with the Bletchley ethos that you didn't ask questions: if you needed to be told, you were told, and if not, you shut up. We didn't mention all this to anyone else in the camp.

In any case, the fact that Hitler's wills had been discovered was common knowledge. I think there had been a news item about them having been discovered, or that they had anyway come to light. They were left in the bunker where the suicides of Hitler, Eva Braun and the Goebbels family took place.* The bunker had been reached first by the Red Army, but to begin with they hadn't realised the importance of the two wills and had left them lying there. It wasn't until quite a while later that it was discovered that these documents existed, and at first, they didn't let anyone else see the documents. [Please note, the memories in this paragraph are not all correct – see box for details.]

> *** Hitler and his wills**
> By 30 April 1945, the Red Army was closing in on the underground bunker in Berlin in which Hitler and others were living. Escape and capture were inconceivable to him. Just two days earlier, Italian partisans had executed Mussolini and his mistress as they tried to escape into Switzerland. Their bodies had been brutalised and strung up for all to see.[1]
>
> And so it was that Hitler committed suicide. Eva Braun, to whom he had been married for just one day, poisoned herself with cyanide. They had first fed the poison to Blondi, Hitler's beloved German Shepherd, as a trial run.
>
> As Rena said, Hitler left a political testament and a personal will. Unsurprisingly, his political testament was vile. Among other things it blamed Jews for the war. It named a successor for Hitler: Admiral Karl Dönitz. Dönitz was head of the Navy and became President. It also expelled Hermann Göring and Heinrich Himmler from the Nazi Party, because they had started negotiating with the Allies. The treachery of Himmler incensed Hitler and is thought to have contributed to his decision to kill himself.[2]
>
> Hitler's personal will acknowledged his marriage to Braun, confirmed that they had chosen suicide and declared that he wished his and his wife's bodies to be burned, immediately. The will named Martin Bormann (Hitler's personal secretary) as his Executor and specified how much of his wealth his family should inherit. Strangely optimistic about his legacy, Hitler also gave instructions that the paintings that he 'owned' (or rather, had mainly stolen) should be used to establish a picture gallery in his hometown of Linz.[3]
>
> Rena's assertion that the wills were found in Hitler's bunker wasn't correct; nor was the idea that the Russians found them and tried to conceal them. Prior to his suicide, Hitler had arranged for his political testament and personal will to be copied and spirited away by three trusted messengers, with three different destinations/recipients. The messengers managed to escape the bunker, and they had quite the adventure (involving boats, a yacht, a plane and truck) trying to get away. Mystery One, in Part Three of this book, goes into this episode in more (fascinating) detail.

I can't remember what the document *looked* like. My feeling is that it was handwritten, in pencil, in old-fashioned German Schrift [script/handwriting], but I remember reading somewhere that Eva Braun had typed it. And why should anyone do a handwritten copy of a typed document? I don't know – I might be misremembering. [Hitler's last private secretary Traudl Junge took down the wills by hand, in the early hours of 29 April, before typing them up. What Rena saw could, therefore, have been the original.][4] I don't think it was signed by Hitler: it was a copy. They wouldn't have given us the original. Again, I can't remember, to be honest!

So, we set out, and we *did* take a long time over it. It was quite a long document, and we typed the translation. [In fact, it wasn't long: the two women just took their time translating it, as Major Oughton had requested!] I can't remember how long it took – several hours – but we discussed it, each word more or less; every nuance and all the alternatives. It was a very *technical* discussion, and we looked up words in every dictionary and reference book in sight.

When we came to the word '*kleinbürgerlich*', we were very puzzled as to how to translate it.* I remember particularly discussing how we should do *that*. The context was that Hitler said he didn't expect his entire fortune to go to his family, but he wanted them to get enough to lead a *kleinbürgerlich* way of life. The dictionary we consulted defined it as 'lower middle-class', but we didn't like the sound of that: we didn't think that 'lower middle-class' had quite the right ring about it. It had a *pejorative* feel, which we didn't think the German had; maybe we were wrong. So, we decided to translate it as 'petty-bourgeois', but we were a bit uneasy about translating a German phrase via French, so we also put *kleinbürgerlich* in brackets.

> * *Kleinbürgerlich*
> The original will did not use the word *kleinbürgerlich* exactly: this is just the plain adjective, not reflecting the variations that the German language uses. Actually, it said: '*zur Erhaltung eines kleinen bürgerlichen Lebens*' ('to maintain a petty-bourgeois standard of living').[5] Rena might or might not have remembered the exact original; *kleinbürgerlich* is just what she and Margery put in brackets in their English translation, as shorthand for the German, which is more of a mouthful!

It was quite a remarkable thing to have translated Hitler's will. I do regard it as a particularly special moment – one of the more interesting bits! I was interviewed for the BBC World Service years later, and they homed in on this translation of Hitler's will and blew it up into something terribly important that I had done, which I didn't think it was. That created quite a stir when it went out on the World Service, with people still getting in touch and asking about it for some time afterwards!

However, to be honest, I never did understand why the job came to *us*. There are so many mysteries about this. We were linguists, but not the most senior people they could have turned to. It was several months after the wills were discovered, and there were certainly other translations available by then, so why ask *us* for another one?* Again, it was one of those things where, you know, you didn't ask. The whole thing that was drummed into you at Bletchley was: if you need to know something, you'll be told, and if you *don't* need to know it, don't ask.

> *** Multiple translations**
> Hitler's wills had already been translated at least twice prior to the personal will landing on Rena and Margery's desk. The first translations were done by a group of German Jewish soldiers in the British Army; the second by American military intelligence. The American versions were filed, with the original personal will, in the US National Archives. The copies were delivered to the British National Archives. In the German Jewish soldiers' version, '*zur Erhaltung eines kleinen bürgerlichen Lebens*' has been translated as 'for maintaining their present standard of living'.[6] This is not an exact translation, but the soldiers were in a hurry. The US translation is more accurate: 'for the maintenance of a small bourgeois household'.[7] This is similar to Rena and Margery's interpretation.
>
> The story of how the wills were found is quite exciting: for details, see Part Three – Mystery One. There, I also examine why Rena and Margery were asked to translate the will when there were other translations available.

I never found out how the will had been discovered and what use was made of the translation – at least, not for a few years. We thought little more about it, until the historian Hugh Trevor-Roper published his book, *The Last Days of Hitler*.* Of course I bought a copy, and of course I knew who Trevor-Roper was – I think, a colonel in Bad Oeynhausen, the headquarters of the Intelligence Corps in Germany. I started reading the book, and when I came to the bit about Hitler's will, I thought *that* sounds familiar; *I* know where this came from, and sure enough it said: 'petty-bourgeois (*kleinbürgerlich*)'.[8] So, this made me realise that Trevor-Roper had used *our* translation: it was the definitive version! There was a certain pride in realising that it had been an acceptable piece of work. However, there was no sense, at that stage, of having taken part in a historic event. We also discovered that Bill Oughton was a great friend of Trevor-Roper. But this still didn't account for why Trevor-Roper needed *another* translation. Any of his staff there could probably have done it, and in fact he was perfectly capable of doing it himself.

When the book came out, I phoned Margery excitedly. At the time, Margery and her family were living in Fulham, and I saw her quite often. She took the news quite calmly – she was distinctly unimpressed – and immediately started talking about our next meeting. I think I told people that I had done the translation once I found it in Trevor-Roper's book, because it was in the public domain. That was in the '50s, I think, so I kept it secret for a decade or so. [In fact, Trevor-Roper's book was published in March 1947, so Rena actually only had to keep the secret for a year and a bit.]

> * **Hugh Trevor-Roper and *The Last Days of Hitler***
> Professor Hugh Redwald Trevor-Roper (1914–2003) – later Baron Dacre of Glanton – was a British historian, intelligence officer and author. At the end of the war, HTR (as I'll refer to him) was tasked with investigating Hitler's death, amid speculation that he had escaped and might even try to take back power. HTR later wrote the best-selling book *The Last Days of Hitler*, based on the final 10 days of Hitler's life. This included an account of the wills being written and dispatched, and of Hitler's suicide. HTR described the two wills together as a 'last advertisement of the Nazi movement'; a 'dignified valediction to the world and a message to later generations', and yet containing 'nothing but the old hollow claptrap'.[9]
>
> The translation of the will that appears in *The Last Days of Hitler* uses the anglicised French, 'petty-bourgeois'. It doesn't have *kleinbürgerlich* in brackets as Rena remembered. The book also describes the will itself as 'the testament ... of the Austrian petty-bourgeois ... the husband of Eva Braun'.[10] So, it uses Rena and Margery's key word not once but twice.

14

Life and Love in Post-war Germany

In a way, I enjoyed my time in Germany. It was, to begin with, pretty awful. The place was in ruins, and you'd go down to Hanover and see buildings with these black crosses on, which meant there were still dead bodies there. There was one that said: 'and here lurks death.'

[At some point in 1946, Rena went on what she described as 'an illegal trip to Berlin'. She recalled:] We travelled overnight (no luxuries such as sleeping cars), spent one day there and travelled back overnight. Berlin was in ruins, but I do remember seeing the Reichstag, which had been destroyed by fire – not as a result of bombing – and what we were told was the entrance to Hitler's bunker.[1] We also ventured into what was the Russian-controlled part of Berlin, which would not have been possible in later days.

In Bad Nenndorf, we lived in houses that had been for the doctors and patients of the old spa. We were two to a room, but of course we didn't have any luxuries; just army furniture. The beds were army-issue, without proper mattresses. There was running water, which of course was a great advance on the camp at Shenley Road, where you had 'the ablutions'! The bedrooms all had hand basins, not used in ordinary houses at the time. That should have been the height of luxury after Nissen huts in an army camp, but the trouble was, there wasn't any *hot* water, nor adequate heating. For baths, we had to go to the building which had been the place where the spa patients had 'taken the waters' and was now the prison for the people being interrogated. There were some empty houses within the camp, so we went out one night and found an open window on one of them. We went in and got hold of bedside tables with drawers in and managed to get them back to our room. They were the only drawers we had.

[In her letter to Agnes MacMorland, Margery described meals at Bad Nenndorf. These, she said, were 'very disorganised' in the early days; at least before the Sergeants' Mess was established. This, she explained, was because 'our mealtimes have to fit in with the GD ones, which are not suitable at all. We manage to eat, though.' GD stood for General Duties. She added: 'The most striking thing about the food, while I'm on the subject, is the amount of butter we get – lashings at every meal.' This would have made a nice change after wartime rationing.

Margery continues: 'We have Saturday afternoon and Sunday off, and transport is arranged for Hanover most nights, and other places, I think, at the week-ends.

On Thursday there was a dance in camp, and we went in force to do a recce of the man position. It is very necessary, as we are not allowed out of Nenndorf village without male escort, and we wanted to know what the situation was going to be like. Our worst fears were realised. There is an acute shortage of women, and we found ourselves dancing with the most appalling GD men. Some of them were alright, of course, but the idea of spending an evening with one of them is quite impossible. I do have a date for tonight with the most dreadful cave-man, but I'm not going – I'm going to escape to Hanover. The I-Corps is of a different type from Bletchley, but not much better. The chap I like best is a tiny fellow about five feet high, which is unfortunate, as although his company is very pleasant, he's not much good as an escort – strong right and all that.'

And now, over to Rena, conducting some difficult international relations.]

I didn't really get to know any Germans, but we had a run-in with the local vet. We found a dog in the basement of the house we were staying in, and the poor little dog, it had obviously been taken from its owner. It was very soft, and its bones deformed. We took it to the local vet to ask for it to be put to sleep and he was on a racket – he was charging us in cigarettes, which was the currency at the time.[2] Well, there weren't ordinary marks – something that was used by service personnel. Anyway, the vet pretended not to understand our German and gave us pills to give to the poor little beast. In the end, we just had to get one of the soldiers to shoot it, because he was not going to give up charging cigarettes for the drugs.

There were many people over there on rackets, so anything you wanted – any services you wanted from the local population – it was cigarettes. That business of using cigarettes as currency was actually affecting the British balance of payments.[3] I forget how they resolved it exactly, but we got vouchers. How they managed to stop the cigarette traffic, I don't know. And I never did discover who smoked those cigarettes!

Of course, things got better and better, and eventually the whole atmosphere was much more relaxed. Yes, it was quite a nice time.

[When Rena mentioned that, eventually, she and her colleagues in Germany had had 'quite a nice time' (notwithstanding the serious nature of her work), I didn't realise the extent of it; at least not until I had the strange honour of going through her possessions after she died. Among these I found a black leather album, packed with photos and postcards from her time in Germany.

The first item (which fell out of the front page as I opened the album) was the bright red, cut-out front of a packet of Craven 'A' Virginia Cigarettes. I turned the small square over, and on the back I found some juicy details. In fact, the album held lots of secrets and humour, often to be found on the backs of things! On the other side of the cigarette packet was the first piece of fun: a hand-written, faux-official note, saying: 'This is to certify that Sgt. Mc. Haggis is a permanent member of the Sgts' mess B.B. S.V. Bad Nenndorf.' Presumably, this note was written when the mess had just been established. I haven't managed to find out what B.B. S.V. stood for. In any case, I'm so glad that this small piece of cardboard was added to the album and didn't slip out over the years, as otherwise, we'd never have known about Rena's alter ego!

Looking at the rest of the album, it seems that Sergeant McHaggis and her friends jumped at the chance to go sight-seeing and to have all sorts of other experiences while they were in Germany. One postcard to her parents mentions that she had got stuck up a mountain railway that day and was off to go sleighing and riding the next day. And, although there are certainly some serious photos, very many are of Rena and her colleagues having a ball, often with a drink and cigarette in hand. On the backs of the photos depicting parties, Rena has scribbled captions such as: 'Drunk? Who, me?' 'Wot! Drunk again!' 'I don't mind if I do!' and 'Easy does it!' There was clearly a lot of socialising with the opposite sex – so 'the man position' must have improved since Margery's letter in the early days.

One possible secret is given up – nearly 80 years later – on the back of a photograph of a smiling young man in British Army uniform. I removed the photo from the album carefully, turned it over, and on the back, what did I find but a hand-written love note, from a soldier about to return home! It said: "To Rena, the only reason I regret leaving BAOR – Frank.' Young love, perhaps; or perhaps he just admired her sleighing skills. We'll never know the story now, and I don't think that Rena would have given it up anyway. Regardless, this glimpse into the experiences of Rena, Frank and the rest of the Germany gang is just glorious: they all look like they had the time of their lives.]

* BAOR Bye

One final treasure from the black album was a heart-felt, signed note from Field Marshal Montgomery. In it, he thanked departing troops for their service. He wrote:

'I feel I cannot let you leave Rhine Army on your return to civil life without a message of thanks and farewell. Together as 21 Army Group we carried through one of the most successful campaigns in history and as BAOR we have laid a firm foundation for the occupation of Germany. It has been our good fortune to be members of this great team. God bless you and God speed.'

Montgomery of Alamein – Field Marshal; Commander in Chief

15

Homewards

I stayed in Germany for over a year, until I was demobbed in December '46. That was about the same time as I had worked at Bletchley Park.

I came back to the UK, but I didn't come back to *London*; I went back to Scotland first, to see my family. I thought about going to *live* in Scotland, but all my friends were in England. By that time, I had relations in Scotland but not friends, and the thought of ditching my friends … well, you can *say* you're going to stay in touch, but you won't. It's always been important to me to go where my friends are.

Back in England, I started looking for jobs all over the place, but the men were all being demobbed and coming back, and quite rightly being given back the jobs they'd held before. I was well qualified, but I couldn't compete – I had an ordinary degree, as I hadn't stayed on to do an honours. I could only say that I was attached to the Intelligence Corps, full stop. I couldn't say what else I had done: nothing about Bletchley; nothing about working in German camps or the level of responsibility I'd had; nothing about Hitler's will. I didn't sound very tempting for an employer! The only marketable skill I could offer was touch typing. It took four months, I think, applying for everything in sight – suitable and unsuitable – but I got absolutely nowhere. It was a very bad time.

I suppose it *was* a bit unfair. I did feel bad at the time, seeing people who were much less well qualified getting jobs ahead of me, and you know, all the *civilians* at Bletchley just walked out after the war, while we were kept in the Army for another 18 months. However, I managed to get on.

16

At the BBC, from the Bottom Up

[Rena did get on, launching her second career, at the BBC. In this era, there weren't many 'career women': there weren't many openings for women at *all*, and most of them got married and had children. This usually meant stopping working, or at least not having the kind of career to which some might otherwise have aspired and been capable. Rena was rather unusual (even among the other Bletchley Park Girls) because she never married nor had children. But was she a sad, 'surplus woman'? Not at all! Right from the word 'go', Rena prioritised professional advancement and her busy social life.

I should mention that Rena's memories of her time at the BBC and onwards were fading when I met her, but she had given interviews years ago which proved very helpful in piecing this part of her story together, along with input from old colleagues.]

When I was in Germany, the NCO, Sean, had taken great interest in my life. It had nothing to do with sex: he thought I had potential. He wrote to me that he'd been speaking to a friend of his who worked in the BBC – what was then External Services (now the World Service).* I didn't know they had one! His friend wrote to me and said he thought I'd enjoy working at Bush House. He advised me to write to the BBC (he gave me the exact address), to say that I wanted to work there, that I could type and would be prepared to take any job that was offered. He said they'd give me a job, and that *that* would give me access to internal advertisements. And that was exactly what I did. I applied for and got a fairly lowly job as a clerk; not quite the bottom grade but very near it. I was jolly glad to get anything! It was at Bush House, in the East European Service of BBC External Services. I thought I could perhaps use my languages there.

> ***The World Service**
> The BBC World Service launched in December 1932, as the BBC Empire Service. Its headquarters were at Bush House in London.[1] Foreign language broadcasts (in Arabic) started in 1938, followed by broadcasts in all major European languages. The organisation was renamed 'The BBC Overseas Service' in 1939, with a BBC European Service added in 1941. Together, these were referred to internally as 'External Services'. Unlike the rest of the BBC, External Services/the World Service was, until 2014/15, funded by the Foreign Office.

The clerk's job was my least favourite at the BBC, but Bush House was very interesting. The offices were not terribly up to date and well organised, and the food wasn't terribly good (but this was 1947 – the food wasn't terribly good anywhere)! However, it was very friendly. There was no pulling of rank or anything: the top brass mixed with the underclass without any distinction. It was all first names, and so on, at a time when people generally didn't use first names. There were lots of very original characters there, and in the canteen, you could hear any language being spoken. [In fact, quite a few staff from Bletchley Park went on to work for the World Service, like Rena.]

I duly looked at the internal advertisements and managed to move into the German Service, on a slightly higher grade. That was a *wonderful* experience. It was quite soon after the war, and during the war, the German Service had been the largest service. It was really an eye-opener, because it was full of people who came over before the war, as refugees, to escape from Hitler, and who had been very distinguished people in their own spheres before they came over. Some of them made names for themselves over here.

The section I was in, within the German Service, was the Features Department. There were two strands to that: the propaganda stuff that was going to East Germany and things like Shakespeare and Ibsen plays for the West Germans.[2] There were a lot of actors about the place. That just couldn't happen now, could it?! But we weren't *setting out* to do propaganda – we were setting out: this is the way we do things, and why don't you come along with us?

Although the job was still quite lowly, it was quite busy! It was mainly typing things, and clearing copyright on some of the things that were going out in programmes. In particular, for anybody on the books as someone who [believed they? – Rena wasn't very clear here] knew about music – I had to get it cleared with the Music Department, run by a man called Lionel Salter.* Lionel always needed to be asked in advance. The people in the German Service would say: 'Oh, that's rubbish!' and I used to get calls from this man (Lionel Salter), and he'd say: 'Miss Stewart, you've done it again!' I was piggy in the middle.

> *** Lionel Salter**
> Lionel Salter was a multi-talented man. His son, Graham, describes him as a: 'pianist, harpsichordist, conductor, arranger, broadcaster, editor, examiner, opera producer, translator, and BBC Assistant Head of Music'. Graham told me: 'My father was known for his encyclopaedic memory and attention to detail (along with his musicianship), so I can understand how matters had to be passed by him before release.' Interestingly (given Rena's story) Graham added that: 'My father taught code breaking, probably before being shipped out to Algeria, where he worked in intelligence, in addition to his 'cover' in education … also acting as Chief Guest Conductor to the Radio France Symphony Orchestra, then in exile in North Africa. He also vetted people arriving home from Dunkirk, as part of his work in intelligence.' Rena was right about there being lots of original characters at Bush House![3]

While I was at Bush House, the Festival Hall opened. That made a great difference to our lives. We didn't have to listen to the Royal Albert Hall echo any more, and it was easy walking distance from the office. There was a young baritone called Fischer-Dieskau who was just coming into prominence at that time. We went to every recital he gave! My favourite piece was *An die Musik*.[4]

I thoroughly enjoyed my time at Bush House. However, I could see there wasn't much of a future for me, because broadcasting was only done by native speakers of the language, and there wasn't very much on offer apart from broadcasting. So I was always trying to convince them that I was worth more, and I kept applying for journalist jobs.

17

Caversham Monitoring Station: Progress and Peril

I tried for a job as a German monitor at Caversham Monitoring Station*, but they had an exam paper with general knowledge questions which were mostly about political things between the wars, which I knew absolutely nothing about. I couldn't answer any of the questions, so I got up and walked out! But I must have made *some* impression, because one day, somebody came into the office and said: 'Would you be willing to go to Caversham as an *English* monitor – holiday relief for six weeks?' and I said: 'Oh yes, I'd welcome that.' I went for six weeks and stayed for ten years!

> *** BBC Monitoring and Caversham Park**
> The 'BBC Monitoring' (BBCM) division of the BBC was established at the start of the Second World War, to monitor broadcasts by the Nazis (and later all enemy and many other foreign broadcasts). It moved into Caversham Park, near Reading, in 1943. BBCM still exists but is now based in New Broadcasting House in central London.[1] Caversham had its own news bureau, which was supplied with information by its monitors. This was a bit like a news agency: items would be sent out by teleprinter to other BBC newsrooms, and on to the news agencies themselves.

I was quite pleased with the English monitor job, because it was considered a kind of fringe journalist job. We were allowed to join the NUJ (the National Union of Journalists) but very much on sufferance. The great thing about the monitoring station was that it was monthly paid, whereas the clerical job was weekly paid. So that was the great leap – from weekly to monthly paid!

The job was really all about listening to foreign broadcasts.* This was for two reasons: one, because you could occasionally get a news item that no-one else had picked up – which didn't happen very often: *Reuters, AFP* [*Agence France Presse*] – they'd all come up with the same thing; and two: to keep people informed of what was happening in those countries.

[By this time, the Cold War was under way, and once again, Rena was involved in secret work. Security at Caversham was tight. In an interview many years later, for a programme on the history of the BBC called *How the BBC Began*, she shared a few details about this. She said:] We had an out-station up a hill, with aerials. There were *some* aerials at Caversham, but they didn't want to have a *lot* of aerials there, because they didn't want the local people to know what was going on there. On the top storeys there was an American unit. Of course they were there purely from an intelligence point of view. They were working for the CIA, telling America what we were doing. I think that was a bit hush-hush, you know![2] ['The Americans' at Caversham Park were the London bureau of the FBIS (Foreign Broadcast Information Service; now called OSE – the Open Source Enterprise). The FBIS had a bureau on the first floor of the building and received items of interest from the BBC monitors.]

> *** Listening to history**
>
> During her time at Caversham, Rena served on the Russia desk. She was tasked with monitoring Soviet broadcasts (albeit all in English: Radio Moscow broadcast in several languages). What Radio Moscow said (including in English) was of huge and often urgent interest to British and US intelligence. It is possible that Rena played a small role in resolving the Cuban Missile Crisis while at Caversham. I investigate this possibility in Part Three – Mystery Three.
>
> However, although Rena would have focused on Russian broadcasts, BBC contacts tell me that it's likely that she would have listened in to radio broadcasts in English from elsewhere in the world, as well. She may well have witnessed local coverage of many significant events, such as the Korean War (1950–1953), the death of Stalin (1953), the Suez Crisis (1956) and the launch of the Sputnik satellite by the Soviet Union in 1957, which sparked the space race.

18

Into the Newsroom

In any case, what I wanted to do all along was news; at that time considered to be a man's job. There was this idea that you couldn't have a *woman* writing about disasters (earthquakes etc). What rubbish! The idea that I couldn't write about disasters without bursting into tears? Nonsense! There were still quite a few women there who had been engaged [hired] during the war, when they couldn't get men. They were mostly coming up to retirement, and when they *did* retire, they were replaced by men.

With no relevant experience or training, I had a hard time convincing the BBC to let me work in news. I spent ten years at Caversham and kept applying for sub-editor jobs but was regularly turned down. My mother was a no-nonsense woman. She backed me up very much, saying: 'Why should you be overlooked because you're female? If you can do the job, get on with it!' [I asked Rena if her parents were proud of her working at the BBC. She said:] My parents had long ago given up trying to understand what I did!

The man in charge at the newsroom in Caversham was a man who thought women were rubbish. One woman got into the newsroom just after the end of the war, and she had a *dreadful* life there! He managed to find fault in her when he wouldn't in a man. I had no ambition to get into *that* kind of newsroom. So yes, there was sexism – I just thought women weren't getting a look-in – but I managed to conquer it somehow. [Nevertheless, as they say, she persisted.][1]

The final job I applied for was for a sub-editor in the newsroom back at Bush House. I thought, *if I don't get this one, I'm just going to settle down and enjoy monitoring.* It was actually a very good life: very pleasant company, meeting interesting people, and a nice place to live in … but that was the application that was accepted! So yes, eventually I made it, in the early '60s. I would have been getting towards 40, and I was rather pleased that I'd got there, in spite of being female.

It was very low-tech in the newsroom; it was entirely spoken news – no inserts, and we didn't have Radio Newsreel at that stage [Radio Newsreel was a World Service programme featuring live news reports from correspondents in the field]. We were also all very conscious of the fact that a lot of it was going out on short wave, and people would have difficulty hearing it. We had devices to make up for that, like mentioning the name of the country or town more than once.

[In the documentary *How the BBC Began*, Rena and her colleagues gave some insights into the life of a news producer at External Services/the World Service. During the programme, John Tusa, a former World Service producer in the '60s, and later World Service Managing Director, recounted that 'A BBC Correspondent in, say, a fairly remote part of Africa would ring up and say: "Such and such has happened," and the response from the duty editor would be: "Very interesting, old boy; I think we'll wait for the second source."' To this, Rena added:] They usually wanted to have two sources for every news story, but of course the trouble was, I remember it was either Northern or Southern Rhodesia ... and we discovered it was the same man who was doing both jobs![2]

There I was, a sub-editor, thinking *this is fine, I'm going to do this and enjoy it*. Then a few vacancies for chief sub-editors came up and I didn't put in for them; I was Johnny-come-lately. The editor came to me and asked: 'Why haven't you applied for Chief Sub?' I said I didn't think there was any point. 'Everybody is applying,' he said. Well, I got it, and then duty editor.

19

Senior Duty Editor, *and* a Woman!

Eventually, I applied for the job as senior duty editor and got it, so I became the first woman to reach the grade of senior duty editor in the World Service – a minor distinction!* There were *some* female sub-editors in Bush House, but the more senior jobs were – until then – all held by men. A *duty* editor was the senior person on that shift. A *senior* duty editor was … oh, I forget … ah, on the *night* shift, the senior duty editor was the most senior person in the building. As senior duty editor, I decided which stories would lead the bulletin. It was a dream job, and that was because of the feeling that I was *female* and doing it! ['Rena,' I had to ask, 'are you a feminist?':] 'Yes, I am!' [she replied with gusto. I really couldn't believe that she was 100 years old!]

[On daily life as a senior duty editor, Rena recalled:] There used to be a morning meeting (and an evening one), where all the senior people in the newsroom met in the editor's office to say their intentions for the rest of the shift. At the time, I was the only woman in there, so the editor said: 'Good morning, gentlemen,' and I said: 'Ken, I'm not a gentleman!' so he said: 'Good morning, gentlemen and Rena.'

Just after I had been promoted, I walked into the newsroom one day. The sub-editors had their desks at the window, looking out onto the Strand. It was the night shift, and a sub came over and said: 'I don't want to worry you, but all the traffic on the Strand has stopped.' This was the time of the Irish bombings. We had some instructions as to what to do, but I hadn't read them, so I said: 'Phone Scotland Yard and ask what they're playing at.' At the time, it was so ridiculous: people thought it great fun to come to the BBC and say that a bomb had been planted. It was mostly rubbish, but you never knew. So, we phoned Scotland Yard, and they said that yes, they *had* stopped the traffic, but that they didn't believe it was a real bomb. It turned out that genuine Irish people didn't like the complainers [hoaxers]. We agreed, through Scotland Yard, to say that if they didn't use the term 'Irish bastard' it wasn't genuine!

I thoroughly enjoyed my time in the newsroom, and I can't see why people thought it was a man's job. [Perhaps they didn't want women thoroughly enjoying themselves!]

* A great boss

One of the people that Rena managed at the BBC, Ian D. Richardson, eventually became a good friend of hers. Ian once asked Rena what her motivation for becoming the first female senior duty editor (SDE) had been. She told him: 'I didn't want to work under [mumble, mumble]' – a very irritating male candidate, thought to have a very good chance of getting the job. This might mean that Rena ended up being the irritating male colleague's boss – how satisfying!

Ian had some interesting recollections on those long-gone years in External Services / the World Service. 'In the early days,' he told me, 'the small number of women journalists in the team included a Polish countess, a Lady with a capital L, a former secretary in the Belgrade Embassy and an openly racist woman who loved the cats in her neighbourhood cemetery, but not any person who wasn't white or English.'

Ian was full of praise for Rena's skills as a journalist, and for her determination not to become an 'imitation bloke'. 'She remained very much her own person and was respected for that,' he said. He asked another of Rena's colleagues, who had joined the newsroom at about the same time as her, what *he* had thought of her. This colleague, Gwyn Jones, recalled that 'Rena's news judgement was always respected, despite her never having been a reporter out in the field.'

Ian added: 'Rena made those working under her feel at ease. Her briefings to the team of writers were simple. As she handed over a fistful of news agency cables and reports from staff correspondents, she would tell the writer what she thought was the main point of the story and the points that should be considered for inclusion. Unlike some other SDEs, who left the writers with little time for creativity, she left writers to produce what they felt was right. The quality of the output very much benefitted from this approach.'

20

On Marriage (and Cracking Glass Ceilings)

[I feel bad cutting away from Rena's distinguished career at this point, to the topic of 'the man position', but I couldn't *not* ask her about that, and about the other M word (marriage). I knew that Rena never married nor had children, but I wondered how she *felt* about that. Luckily, she didn't mind being asked (though she didn't talk about feelings or children, and I didn't push). She said:] I think I always thought I would marry in the end, but I made a private arrangement with myself to focus on my career. I was also concerned that there were certain jobs that were 'men's jobs', and I wanted to do them. It's a very small distinction now, when BBC News has many women in senior posts, but I'd say I didn't break the glass ceiling, but I made a few cracks!

21

Time Out

[Footloose and fancy free in terms of the man position, what did fun-loving Rena do with her spare time? Well, for one thing, she travelled extensively. I can imagine that that was unusual when she was younger, especially for a woman. I asked her if she travelled with work, but she replied:] I didn't really travel abroad with the World Service, but I did have a sabbatical for two months. The BBC said: 'You *could* stay at home and cut the grass, but really we'd like you to travel abroad; visit some of the countries we cover.' I thought: *for the first month, I have two people in Canada I could visit. For the second month, I really ought to go somewhere else.* And I thought: *I'll be across the Atlantic anyway, so why not Mexico?* It was coming up to the time to go, and I thought: *you're mad! You don't speak the language, and you don't know a <u>soul</u>.* Thank goodness for my dear friend Jean Mackie. We'd been out to see a play in London, and we were going down into the Underground when she said to me: 'Can I come to Mexico too?' 'Yes!' I said.

I met Jean at the airport in Mexico, as I'd been in Canada. I remember she had a case with wheels. That was very up to date! We had a great time, and because it was close to the States, everybody spoke English. We travelled around, and it was *hot*. There were all these Inca trails ... [At this point, Rena trailed off (excuse the pun!) Sadly, her memory of this trip wasn't complete any more. Her earlier memories were much clearer than her later ones. It is funny the small details that people *do* remember, though; a wheelie suitcase being a good example!

I only realised the extent of Rena's adventures when going through her belongings after she died. Her travels took her all over the UK, and to locations as far-flung as the Soviet Union (for which I found her visa) and various locations in Asia and Asia Pacific, including Tashkent in what is now Uzbekistan. In the 1950s, Rena went on holiday with a friend, Margaret Wesley, who worked with her at BBCM at Caversham, to what is now Croatia. Margaret's son Peter sent me a beautiful photo of Rena sitting by the sea. He also sent one of her with a donkey, but that one's not quite as glamorous so it didn't make the cut for her biography!]

22

Retirement

I worked at the BBC for 36 years. I retired in 1983 and was sad to leave, so I've now been retired for 40 years, which is longer than I worked there!*

Although I was sad, I was quite ready to have fun. I love going to theatres, travel and music, though my piano playing was pathetic! However, even if you play badly, I think it does help to *try* and play well.

[I asked Rena if she still used her German.] The only German I use is … well, I'm very fond of German *Lieder* [songs that set poetry to music].[1] I can understand what they're singing.

[Rena was later invited back to Bush House (near Waterloo Bridge) as a special guest for the final broadcast of a radio news bulletin from the building. This took place on 12 July 2012. The World Service would then move to Broadcasting House, near Oxford Circus. Andrew Whitehead, a BBC colleague of Rena's whose interview of Rena has been amalgamated into this book, was present, and he recalled how pleased he had been that she was able to be there. Rena reflected, at the time of her visit:] Bush House gave me a very interesting life, and I made some very good friends there. But it's just very sad that it's moving. I can't think the atmosphere there is going to be recreated in the new newsroom, because the domestic services didn't think very much of us, and we didn't think very much of them. [Office politics is clearly not a new thing!]

---

* **Comments from Rena's colleagues on her retirement**, written in a beautiful, monogrammed leather album, embellished with the coat of arms of the BBC and its motto: *Nation Shall Speak Peace Unto Nation*.

- 'Young Rena can't really be retiring, it must all be a leg-pull.'
- 'You've been a tower of strength and your good humour has been an example to us all.'
- 'Now who can I look to to keep pace with The Times of the day?'
- 'We'll miss you and your steadying influence.'
- 'I fear the newsroom is going to become more frenetic, but less interesting!'

- 'One fewer voice of sanity in the newsroom.'
- 'You'll be remembered as quietly professional and, even more, one of the nicest people of all to work with.'
- 'Well, they did say women would never stand the pace! All I can say is what a wonderful example you've set us gals – it won't be forgotten.'
- 'Unlike our first female PM, Rena, you've done us proud as the first female SDE.'
- 'You will be an impossible gap to fill.'
- 'It's 03:20 Rena, and I can't think of anything to say except how delicious it must be for you to look forward to years of being asleep at this ungodly hour.'

23

Back to Bletchley

[Having read this far, it won't come as a surprise to you to learn that Rena had a busy retirement. Among other things, she went back to Bletchley Park many times, from the time it became a museum, in 1994. She last visited at the ripe old age of 95.]

I did learn things, visiting the museum at Bletchley, that I didn't know at the time. For example, the reason we were in the Army was because they'd run out of civilian billets!* To begin with, they were able to knock on people's doors and see if someone had a bedroom unused, and if so, ask if they could billet four people working at the Park. But then there was a big increase in the volume of [radio] traffic at Bletchley at that time, and they needed more staff. All the civilian billets around Bletchley were full, so they hastily built an army camp on Shenley Road, adjacent to the Park, and we were one of the first people to go there. People had *horror* stories about billets, but that was nothing compared to the horror of the camp!

> *** Billets to barracks**
> Rena didn't say who told her this story, but it's not quite as straightforward as she was told. Dr Cheetham explained: 'Recruiting policy took months to have an effect, and there were lots of factors other than accommodation. But Rena does allude to one of the big motivations for employing service people at Bletchley Park: it meant that [Bletchley] could offload the cost and administration onto someone else!'

When I was a visitor in the early days of the museum, I got to know Tony and Margaret Sale well. [Tony and Margaret were involved in setting the museum up.][1] Tony once invited me to come in, and he had a recording machine. He said: 'Just talk.' The trouble was that most of the things we talked about were the things that happened in the *camp* and not Bletchley Park. I don't think he got an awful lot out of that!

I had a phone call a few years ago from the only one of my German Book Room colleagues who was alive then; Elma Wasmoeth, who *was* Elma Morley.

She phoned me around the time of the annual reunion to see if I was thinking of going, and we had quite a long chat. I was at the stage where I couldn't really use public transport, and I dropped hints all round, but nobody took them up!

[Recalling a trip to Bletchley when the then Duchess of Cambridge (now Princess of Wales) paid an official visit, Rena made me laugh out loud. Her verdict was:] Well, *that* was a waste of time! I took Jan [our mutual friend] to the museum. We finished up in a room in the mansion. The people with us were sitting at the end of the room. There were four of us veterans. The first one was a woman who kept talking and talking and talking! I spent 20 minutes looking at Kate's back. The woman had worked in the Telegraph Room. I didn't know such a place at the time, because of the secrecy. And they said to me: 'Did *you* work in the Telegraph Room as well?' and I said: 'No,' but before I could say anything else, I got cut off!²

In about 2009, we were all given a medal by a grateful government. It came with a letter signed by Gordon Brown, who was prime minister at the time. It thoroughly annoys me! It came from GC&CS – the Government Code and Cypher School.* Well, I never heard Bletchley Park called *that* while I was there! It has on it 'Bletchley Park and Outstations', and on the back, it says: 'We also served.' What's the 'also' for? Of *course* we served! What did they think we were *doing*? I much prefer the brooch I have, which just says something like 'Bletchley Park Veteran'. So no, I didn't write back to Gordon Brown and thank him.³

> *** GC&CS who?**
> The Government Code & Cypher School (GC&CS) pre-existed Bletchley Park: it was an army and naval signals intelligence organisation, established in 1919. Bletchley Park was simply its top-secret base during the war, and the acronym was perhaps only communicated on a need-to-know basis. Presumably, Rena didn't need to know! The organisation carried on after the war. It's now known as GCHQ (Government Communications Headquarters) and is based in Cheltenham.⁴

24

Songs (and Dances) of Praise

[Rena reflects on three important threads in her life, which often overlapped: the Church, music and Scottish culture/dancing.]

The Church has been a big part of my life, and a guide. I *was* Church of Scotland but not any more – I'm now United Reformed. [Rena appeared in a special *Songs of Praise* feature on Bletchley Park – possibly her greatest moment, bar getting the SDE job?! She told them:] I think that for anyone who has lived through a war, peace becomes even more important. I'm very fond of the hymn *Make me a channel of your peace*, which uses the words of St Francis of Assisi.[1]

> **Rena's Desert Island Discs**
> Speaking of music, in 2014, Rena's local branch of u3a (the University of the Third Age) in Ealing invited her to present her 'desert island discs' – that is, the pieces of music that she would want to be able to listen to if she were a castaway on a desert island. The event wasn't in exactly the same format as the BBC programme of the same name but is a pleasure to watch/listen to. You can find it on YouTube.[2] Rena chose seven great pieces, saying that she had a real preference for choral music. These (most of which will now seem familiar) were:
>
> 1: *Gypsy Rondo*, by Haydn (a reminder of her childhood)
> 2: *La Mer (The Sea)*, by Charles Trenet (which made Rena recall camp life at Bletchley Park)
> 3: *An die Musik (To Music)*, by Dietrich Fischer-Dieskau (evoking visits to the Festival Hall in London)
> 4: *Duetto buffo di due gatti (Humorous duet for two cats)*, by 'G. Berthold' (Robert Lucas de Pearsall) (simply because Rena loved cats, and because she had a gentle sense of humour)
> 5: *Scherzo No. 2 in B-Flat Minor Op. 31*, by Chopin (a recording from the St Barnabas Chopin Festival 2010, played by Rena's friend, Hugh Mathers)

> 6: *Morgen!* (*Tomorrow!*) by Richard Strauss, sung by Felicity Lott and accompanied by Graham Johnson (an example of the German *Lieder* that Rena so loved) and
> 7: *Auld Lang Syne*, sung by Jean Redpath – though Rena was keen to emphasise that this was not the best-known but the *original* tune, which Robert Burns chose for it. She said: 'It's not a story about a boozy party ending; it's about two old men who were very good friends, lost touch with each other, found each other again and were glad to see each other but regretted the wasted years in between.' Rena also mentioned Jean Redpath; that she and her sister Isobel were friendly with her, through their participation in Scottish cultural activities (singing and dancing).

I've been involved in St Andrew's Church in Ealing for many years. [The St Andrew's church website says that Rena had been involved 'as an elder and in many other roles'; and that she 'led the Scottish Country Dance group'.[3] Her nephew, Stewart Maclennan, told me: 'She retired from teaching Scottish dancing (never mind otherwise participating!) only after her 90th birthday,' and that 'another great enthusiasm, shared with my mother, was the Stewart Society.' Sergeant McHaggis' Scottishness was very important to her, even though she lived in England for most of her life!

Continuing on the Scottish theme, the St Andrew's website adds that Rena was 'famous for the Scottish cakes and delicacies she and her sister Isobel used to make for Burns Suppers and other festive occasions'. I asked Rena about this, and she admitted that she wasn't a good *cook*, but she did describe herself as 'rather a good baker'. *The Great British Bake Off* missed a chance to feature its first centenarian!]

25

A Significant Celebration

I had my 100th birthday party at a church – St Mary's Perivale. I've got a video of it! That church isn't used as a church any more. Well, it hasn't been *deconsecrated*, but it's used for concerts. [Stewart Maclennan said that Rena (when aged 99) had insisted on organising her party herself, pitting her iron will against his desire for her not to overdo it, but that the party nevertheless went 'tremendously well'.]

[The website of Rena's own church, St Andrew's, said of the party: 'It was a joyous occasion. Family and friends from the many areas of Rena's life mingled midst beautiful flowers to toast Rena, enjoy her spectacular birthday cake and admire her card from King Charles and his wife.' Rena recalled:] I got my letter from King Charles. I can't remember when … It suddenly turned up at my party!

[The website continues: 'Rena's nephew spoke fondly of his early memories of his aunt, and we were reminded of modest Rena's many achievements. She has featured in several television documentaries in recent years, and a representative from Bletchley Park came to thank her for her service to the country.' The website mentions that one of her former staff from the BBC came along and said what a great boss she was!]

[I asked Rena what the secret is to reaching 100. I was interested because I've read many inspirational accounts from other centenarians on this question, with answers ranging from eating Shredded Wheat to living by the seaside. Perhaps, I mused, the secret might be Scottish dancing. However, according to Rena it's simply to 'keep on breathing'. *Quite right*, I said to myself, and typically Rena. She wasn't one for being soppy, and in my opinion, that's OK.]

26

A Significant Achievement

[Rena had already told me what she was most proud of in her 100 years of life: getting the job as senior duty editor at the World Service, as a woman. She later added:] My greatest achievement has been getting people to recognise that a woman can be as good a journalist as a man. I'd like to be remembered as a good journalist. [I aim to make sure of this!]

27

Creature Comforts

[We're coming towards the end of Rena's story now, and I couldn't omit to mention Rena's love of cats, and of her caring friends.

On the topic of cats, she reported, some years ago:] I adopted a cat the *moment* I retired. Up 'til then, I'd depended on seducing other peoples' cats and leaving *them* to clear out the litter trays! I thought it was time I had a cat of my own. My sister's cat had kittens at just about that time, and I got a very nice tabby kitten – a very *successful* cat. I'm now on my third cat; a beautiful tortoiseshell called Judy. She's thoroughly spoiled – that's what you get a cat for![1]

[One of the loveliest aspects of visiting Rena was meeting Judy the cat. At the time of my last visit, Judy was 18 years old. That made her an old lady too, but a mere 88 human years, compared to Rena's 100! On my final visit before Rena died, Judy was particularly sprightly and keen for affection. She sat with us while we talked, occasionally advancing a cautious paw towards one of the Scottish oatcakes that Rena was eating, and hoping that we wouldn't notice! I promised Rena that Judy would feature in her biography, and she was pleased about that.

Rena still lived at home but had a carer. For many years, her carer (and great friend) was Lidine Winter, whom I thought it important to mention and thank. Rena also had our mutual friend next door, Jan. Jan was forever popping over to help Rena and was very fond of her. It was certainly a comfort to Rena to have Judy the cat, Lidine, Jan and others nearby.

28

… and a Celebration of a Life Well Lived

And now here we are, at the end of Rena's epic, 100-year journey. As mentioned, Rena was starting to lose her memory, so it seemed likely that she'd fade away slowly. Sadly, that wasn't to be. She fell ill suddenly and died in the morning of 11 November. How apt for a veteran to go on Armistice Day. Thankfully, she had friends at her bedside, and she seemed quite peaceful.

Stewart said how delighted his aunt would have been to know that she was honoured with not one but *two* bumper newspaper obituaries (both a decent length and befitting such a person of note). One was in *The Times*, whose crossword Rena did every day, and one in *the Guardian*, which, as a life-long Labour voter, was apparently 'her' paper.[1] The many comments from readers in the online versions are a pleasure to read.* Apparently randomly, Rena also received an obituary in an Italian newspaper – *La Stampa* – which itself was then picked up by several others in Italy.[2] I wasn't sure why this would be, as she didn't have particular links to Italy. I mentioned the unexpected obituary to Stewart, who reflected: 'Italy is a country which – its present government notwithstanding – still gives due honour to all who helped liberate it from fascism and Nazism.' I was pleased to hear this.

Then came Rena's funeral, at St Andrew's Church in Ealing. This was the most celebratory funeral I've ever attended. Rena gave new meaning to the concept of having 'had a good innings'. I suppose, like any other funeral, it brought together lots of people from her life who might have known some, but not all, of her story. However, all were in particular awe of this wonderful woman, and of everything she packed in to her life. I think she would have enjoyed the funeral (but been a bit embarrassed)! We sang *Make me a channel of your peace*, and then the funeral finished with a recording of the beautiful version of *Auld Lang Syne* which she so loved. As was entirely appropriate, Rena was then conveyed back home to Scotland. She now rests in peace at Largo Parish Church, Fife, with her parents. I hope to pay my respects to her there sometime soon.]

* 'A huge inspiration': selected comments from readers of Rena's obituaries in *The Times* and *the Guardian* (some paraphrased)

- 'Now THAT'S how to live a life. Bravo!'
- 'A lady who knew what she wanted and did it! RIP.'
- 'Fascinating, and that's just what we know about. Honestly, we need a few more of the likes of Rena Stewart, with her acumen and attention to detail.'
- 'Stories like this lift my spirits. It's a pleasure to be reminded of our good fortune, due in large part to people like Rena Stewart.'
- 'The debt we owe this generation is incalculable. What an amazing woman.'
- 'She had such an exciting life – I wish the BBC would make a drama about her.'
- 'Thank you for your service, ma'am.'
- 'Three words darling – a ma zing. What a lady.'

Part Two

Remembering Rena's Bletchley Friends

Some of the best friendships are formed in adversity – even if that adversity involves tedious typing and compulsory PE. Rena made strong, life-long friendships at Bletchley Park. She clearly cared deeply about Agnes, Elma and Margery, and their stories complement each other. Therefore, I felt it appropriate to commemorate those friends here as well – with the permission of their proud families.

First, however, I had to track their families down! I sleuthed around a bit on Facebook and LinkedIn, but it was proving tricky, until I discovered that Rena had a Facebook page. *Good old Rena*, I thought, *didn't she go with the times*! Even then, it wasn't clear who all her connections were, nor if any were related to Agnes, Elma and Margery. I decided to contact as many possible relatives as I could, in the hope that at least one per friend would respond. I did manage to connect with each of the three families eventually, and I asked them if they'd be willing help with a short biography and some photos. Luckily, they agreed.

There were a couple of surprises, though. I had assumed that Rena was the last of the four, but she wasn't: Agnes was still alive at the time, and 101 years old! Sadly, she died a few months later; the last of the gang. Elma had died a few months previously, just short of her 100th birthday, so that was two, almost three, centenarians out of four. Quite impressive! Poor old Margery died much younger, and her story had a bit of a twist in it – but let's start with A for Agnes.

1

Agnes Glynn (née Gardner)

By Martin Glynn and Andrea Stone (Agnes' son and granddaughter)

Agnes was born Agnes Cunningham Gardner in Cellardyke, Fife, Scotland, on 6 September 1922. Cellardyke is a small village on the East Neuk of Fife, on the northern shores of the Firth of Forth, about 50 miles north of Edinburgh. In those days it was a thriving fishing community, nestled next to Anstruther, a bigger, more prosperous town and about nine miles from St Andrews. Agnes' father, Martin Gardner, was a fisherman, well recognized in the town, and at one point coxswain of the local lifeboat. His nickname was 'Acorn Mairt,' in recognition of the name of his fishing boats. Her mother, born Agnes Ann Thomson, was a devoted fisherman's wife who focused on the upbringing of her children, Betty, Agnes and Henry.

The Gardner family lived simply, were God-fearing folk and prospered in their world of East Fife. Agnes emerged quickly as being somewhat different, as she was keen on school and wanted to pursue other areas of interest. She loved her upbringing and the extended family, where multiple generations lived in their home. She was bosom buddies with her sister Betty, getting into all kinds of trouble and fun things. Besides being a strong student, a highlight was being captain of the girls' field hockey team at the Waid Academy in Anstruther. Agnes' strong Christian faith emanated from her roots, believing in standing up for what is right and generosity of spirit, with hypocrisy being the biggest sin.

In spite of the world being at war, Agnes left for the University of St Andrews, where she took languages – particularly French and German. As there was no money to spare, she commuted from home for the first two years and stayed in a house on Largo Road for the final year. She loved it at St Andrews and made a number of new friends. These included Rena Stewart, whom she met on the first day, when registering. The war was difficult on the whole region, with Agnes' father off in the Navy and her sister to England, commanding a searchlight group.

Having graduated in 1943, Agnes wanted to contribute to the war effort. As many avenues were closed, she applied for a role in the Auxiliary Territorial Service, or ATS, but was assigned to work in intelligence. As she said, it was a special posting that no one knew about, but off she went for an interview. After proving her proficiency in German she was off to Bletchley Park, after six weeks of training in Surrey. Bletchley Park, the home of 'Ultra', was a fascinating place but, as everyone was sworn to secrecy, it was only discovered later how important it was to the war effort. Agnes' university friend Rena arrived at Bletchley at the same time, and they quickly met Elma Morley (later Elma Wasmoeth), to become a trio of best friends from Scotland.

Agnes recounts the austere living conditions in the huts at the Park, the fun hitchhiking trips into London and the hard work documenting and decoding German intelligence messages. As she said, she saw the war from the German side, and she got to know the personalities and expressions of tank commanders and army units as they discussed strategies and gossip! When the war ended, British intelligence, particularly MI5, was in as much demand as ever, and Agnes and her mates were sent to Bad Nenndorf in Germany, dealing with prisoners and spies of all kinds.

While in Germany, a young sergeant in a tank regiment, named Hubert, asked Agnes out on a date. As Hubert was a proficient horse rider and had the chance to exercise some horses, he asked her to go riding. She said yes, even though she had never really ridden, and halfway through she fell off and broke her arm. Needless to say, this was awkward for Hubert, and he had no choice but to see her again. They got married in February 1948.

Where should this couple settle down and live permanently was the question. After several short-term jobs in London, and with each having university degrees but no money, they put out applications to various places and settled on Canada. After two years in a pulp and paper town in northern Ontario called Marathon, they moved to Montreal, where Hubert found a job with British Petroleum. Agnes chose not to work full time, as Martin was born in 1951. Life was happy in Montreal, with lots of friends, an active church life and many back-and-forths to Scotland, England and sometimes Europe. Hubert's parents lived in London, and many family members lived in Germany as well. After a dozen years, Hubert got a job in the federal government and off they went to Ottawa. In Ottawa, Agnes ended up pursuing a career as a social worker with the Children's Aid Society. Upon retirement they became 'snowbirds' and lived six months of the year in Clearwater Beach, Florida, playing tennis and swimming every day.

Martin, in the meantime, had moved to Vancouver and had three children: Andrea, John and Harry. The allure of grandchildren was too strong to resist, and the snowbirding continued, but with six months in the Vancouver area, which eventually became 12 months. Hubert passed away in 2000. Agnes lived an active life in her home in Ocean Park near Vancouver, with lots of interaction with grandchildren and friends. She then decided to move into an independent living home called Tapestry, in Vancouver, where she lived until her passing. In the meantime, a new grandson, Aiden, was born in 2009 and three great grandchildren came along: Luke in 2015, Ava in 2017 and Kaia in 2023. There was nothing in her life more important to her than her family, and the addition of great grandchildren brought her more joy.

There is no doubt that Agnes had a full and inspiring life. She passed away peacefully on 25 February 2024, in the care of a wonderful caregiver, Vilma Ibarra, who was critical to her quality of life in her last few years. The Glynn family are extremely grateful for Vilma's tremendous dedication and efforts on Agnes' behalf.

2

Elma Wasmoeth (née Morley)

By Ellie Wasmoeth (Elma's daughter)

Elma Morley was born on 24 October 1923, in a little Scottish village called Uphall, 12 miles west of Edinburgh. She was warmly welcomed as the fifth child of James Morley and Elisabeth (Bessie) Miller. Her brother, Jim, had died after being kicked by a horse and developing septicaemia; her sister, Elsie, died of the Spanish Flu – both at the age of 10. There were no antibiotics in those days, unfortunately. Elma's sister Irene was nine years older, and Sadie 14. This meant that they loved teaching her to read before school did. They taught her poetry and even foreign languages. Later on, she would enter poetry recital competitions and win books and a watch.

Primary school was in Uphall, where Elma's father worked as an engineer for Scottish Oil. He was also an elder in church. They lived in a house owned by Scottish Oil. Every week, wood was delivered to keep the six fires burning, as well as the fire for the washing. Elma was a happy child, loved her mum and dad, who were loving, fair and kind, and she loved her sisters. There were big family gatherings at New Year, with her cousins. Elma had a strong sense of belonging. She enjoyed going to school and was lucky that the girl next door was in her class and a good friend too. Elma started secondary school in Broxburn and then did the last two years at George Watson's in Edinburgh, a private school. Here she met her lifelong friend Mima Peden, who would later work at Bletchley as one of the many civilians there.

Elma went to Edinburgh University, where she studied English Literature, Geography and German. The war had started by then, and as soon as she was 21, she joined the ATS (Auxiliary Territorial Service) and went down to Bletchley Park. She became a sergeant major and worked in the German Book Room with Rena Stewart, where her language skills came in very handy! Rena and Elma became very good friends, though neither of them had a clue what the other was doing. Of course, we now do: Elma was typing the decoded messages from the Germans, as was Rena. These messages often started with a saying, just to see if the line was working.[1] For example: *'Alles hat ein Ende, nur die Wurst hat zwo'* (Everything has an end; only a sausage has two) or *'Die Liebe ist ein Omnibus, auf den man ewig warten muss, und komt er endlich angewetzt, dan ruft der Schaffner, Schon besetzt'* (Love is like a bus: you have to wait forever for one, and when it finally gets there, the bus conductor says it's already full).

The accommodation at Bletchley was Nissen huts.[2] The people worked in three shifts, and so the beds were used three times as well! The ablutions were far from ideal, and scabies was not uncommon. One time on leave, Elma went straight to the family's trusted house doctor, Dr MacAlpine, who would always have great remedies. He could instil faith and trust in you, which, in itself, already helped with many symptoms.

People really had no idea what was going on at Bletchley, but this contributed to creating a strong community with great friendships. Elma formed very strong friendships with people like Rena Stewart, Aggie Gardner, Margery Forbes and Dorothy Donaldson.[3] One time, she and Aggie were hitching down from London after leave. They got a lift from Glenn Miller (the famous band leader)'s driver, who took them right back. Another time, they were punting near Oxford. As Elma had one leg on the jetty, the boat started drifting off. Of course, this was in front of a pub garden, with lots of people watching. She could make one of two choices: either head first or feet first. She chose the latter, accompanied by loud cheering, of course! Her uniform utterly soaked, they went back to Bletchley.

Another time, they had to stand for inspection, and the officer in charge poked at the unfastened top of the breast pocket of her jacket, lifted it up and said: 'Sunbathing?' Elma was called 'Sunshine' in the Sergeants' Mess: she always had a keen sense of humour and a kind heart. This remained so her entire life!

After the war ended, many from Bletchley went to Bad Nenndorf in Germany. Here they worked at the prisoner of war camp. Elma's work consisted of typing out the interrogations of the prisoners. This was really a very happy part of her life; the war over, together with many close friends, and lots of jolly parties. There were also escapades to the Russian part of Berlin to get stockings!

In 1948, Elma got leave to go to her father, who was dying at 75, leaving her mother a widow at 65. Edinburgh University had granted her a War Masters, so she didn't have to go back there. She went to Moray House, a teacher training college in Edinburgh, and taught in several very poor schools.

She later went by boat to Canada to stay with her sister, Sadie, who was a teacher there, and she worked there as a secretary. Just before she left for Canada, she had met a Dutchman, Ton Wasmoeth, at a university camp in Norway. Elma and Ton kept in touch and got married in 1953 in Scotland.

After the war, job opportunities seemed better in Australia, so they emigrated. However, Perth was hot and dry, and alas, this Scottish lass missed the green pastures, and even the rain! Besides, job opportunities weren't as great as they had expected. So, when she was pregnant with her first son, Jack, they returned to The Hague. Elma worked at the International School until the baby was born. Ten months later, Maarten arrived, and then after four years, Ellie.

The family moved regularly, due to Ton's different jobs. He had studied Economics and Sociology and became a head of Human Resources; later he had a consultancy. Ton hadn't had the warm upbringing that Elma had had, so she was the warm and fun centre of the family, and Ton, the hard-working father, with higher demands of his children – always wanting the very best for them. Living out in the country, having goats, a big vegetable garden, making jam and having bees all became very important in the '70s. Ton and Elma instilled this connection with nature into their children.

For Elma, Scotland was always in her heart. She taught her children poetry and songs; they knew more English/Scottish than Dutch songs. She went to Scotland every year at least once: her mother, who had a heart condition, couldn't travel. At home in Holland, she would speak a beautiful mixture of both Dutch and English; sometimes in the same word.

After Ton stopped working, he went to university to study law. They still had another 30 great years together. As they both had a very keen intellect and a sharp mind, they always had so much to talk about. They would share poems and reminisce about the past; talk about books. Elma's memory was amazing, as was Ton's knowledge.

At the end of her life, as Elma knew the time was coming, she phoned up her two Bletchley friends, Rena and Aggie, to thank them for their friendship and wish them well. Ton had died only 10 weeks earlier.

She often said, with gratitude: 'I have had my innings. I have had a good life, great parents, sisters, husband, children and friends.' Elma died on 28 June 2023.

3
Margery Tarwinska (née Forbes)

Based on an article by Graeme Strachan at *The Courier* newspaper, Dundee, with help from Ed Tarwinski (Margery's son)[1]

Margery Lilian Tarwinska (née Forbes) was born in Dundee in 1923, to Charles and Lilian Forbes. She had two brothers: an older brother, Stewart, and a younger one, Harry. Margery had fond memories of childhood holidays, swimming and cycling with her friends. This included cycling from Dundee to Lower Largo (approximately a two-hour ride). Lower Largo just happens to be next door to Lundin Links, where Rena grew up. So, while Rena left Lundin Links to go to Glen Lyon for her holidays, Margery was going the other way! However, it was only at St Andrews that the two first met.

Margery studied languages at St Andrews University and was intelligent, reserved, and with a passion for cryptic crosswords and puzzles. The latter was apparently one of the selection criteria for the Bletchley talent hunters! Although Margery and Rena had met at university, it was on enlisting in the Auxiliary Territorial Service (ATS), in November 1943, and while serving in the German Book Room at Bletchley Park, that their friendship blossomed. They would remain together for the rest of their time in the military.

Margery and Rena were both sent to Bad Nenndorf in Germany at the end of the war. Here they translated the statements of suspected Nazis and war criminals. They then worked together on the translation of Hitler's private/personal will, which later featured in Intelligence Corps officer and historian Hugh Trevor-Roper's book *The Last Days of Hitler*.

Margery and Rena were demobilised in 1946, and Margery went home to Dundee. During the war she had met Marian Jozef Tarwinski, a tank driver, engineer and member of the Free Polish Army, who had been serving in Scotland. They married on her return in 1947. Marian and Margery had three children: Wanda (1948), Rena (1954) and Edmund (1956). The family migrated to Ontario, Canada, in 1957 and then to Ohio, USA, in 1959. Marian sadly died of heart failure in 1962, and Margery returned to Dundee with her children. She found work as a (popular) teacher of languages, at Harris Academy and

Morgan Academy, until 1972. However, she succumbed to cancer in February 1973, aged just 49.

At the time of her death, Margery was still bound by the Official Secrets Act (information about Bletchley was declassified in the mid-1970s). This meant that during her lifetime she was not able to tell her family what she did in the war; only that it was a secret. Just a few years after her death, the information was declassified, and books appeared about Bletchley Park – what had gone on there and what was achieved. Still, Margery's children knew nothing about their mother's involvement.

The truth only came to light in around 1995, and by pure chance. Margery's son Edmund explains that: 'During the course of my business, I had an appointment to visit a lady in Ravelston, Edinburgh. Miss Morley, intrigued by my surname Tarwinski (spelled using the masculine version of Tarwinska, according to Polish convention that our family still follows), asked me what my mother's first name was. When I replied with 'Margery', Miss Morley excitedly revealed that she and my mother had been close colleagues and good friends during the war, and she proceeded to produce a box of photographs and mementos.'

Ed continues: 'This was quite a moment for me, as I had never before met one of my mother's old friends. And this, as far as I recall, was when I first learned that my mother worked at Bletchley Park. After showing me a selection of fascinating photos and other keepsakes, Miss Morley then told me that the person I should really speak to would be Rena Stewart. Apparently, Rena and my mother were best buddies during and after the war, and Rena would have more stories, photos and mementos. It later turned out that my late sister Rena, who sadly died in 2013, was named in honour of Rena Stewart.'

Ed thanked Elma for the revelations and got in touch with Rena, who was living in west London and had retired, after her post-war career at the BBC World Service. He recalls: 'After a number of letters and copies of documents and photos were exchanged, we both filled in the gaps in our knowledge of Margery's life during and after the war. I managed to visit Rena in 1996, where more stories were related, and photographs dug out. And so it was through Rena that I learned of the Hitler's will story, which is a strange one, but guaranteed as a show-stopper at dinner parties!'

Ed, his sister Wanda, and his sister Rena (before she died) have all visited Bletchley Park at various times, where Margery has her own brick in the memorial Codebreakers' Wall. Ed reflects: 'We are very proud of her being selected for the very important work that was done at Bletchley Park, and also the fact that she kept the secret safe, even from her own family.'

Part Three

Three Mysteries

And now for the third and final part of the book: three mini historical mysteries that came to light while I was checking the details of Rena's story. By chance, these latch on neatly to three of the most significant periods of her life: Bletchley Park, Germany and the BBC. However, I've written them in the order in which they arose. I've thoroughly enjoyed delving into all of them: it's amazing how one small question can open a door into so much history *and* turn you into a part-time detective!

Mystery One

Bill, Hugh, and Hitler's Wills

1

The Mystery

You might have thought that this book was just about Rena and her friends. So did I! But when I started out, I had no idea about the terrific tale of Bill, Hugh and Hitler's wills. You'll remember that Major Oughton was Rena and Margery's boss in Germany, and that Hugh Trevor-Roper (HTR) investigated Hitler's fate and the location of his wills. As I was finishing the first draft of the biography, I went through checking historical details and adding explanations where needed. When I came to look up Major Oughton, there was very little to find. The only information that I could see initially was a short mention in the few available articles about Rena and Margery. Perhaps I shouldn't have been surprised, given that Bill was an officer in the Intelligence Corps. Still, it felt a little odd, considering how much the Second World War and its aftermath have been pored over.

I like a challenge, so I decided to try to find out more about Major Oughton, but not before doing a quick search for HTR. And that's when this small query got interesting. On HTR's Wikipedia page, I was amazed to read a particular detail about his investigation into Hitler's fate. It said that while HTR was interviewing and preparing questions for officials who had been in the bunker with Hitler, he used an alias: the name 'Major Oughton'.[1] *How odd*, I thought! *Rena described Bill and Hugh as 'great friends', but could they have been one and the same person?* And *might I even have uncovered some big secret?*

Rena was still alive at this point, so I decided to go back to ask her if Bill and Hugh were one or two. I was curious to see how she might react; whether the news might even prompt her to reveal 'The Big Secret'. In the event, she looked alarmed, exclaiming: 'I'm shocked … I don't believe it!' That was sufficient evidence for me of Bill and Hugh *not* being the same person, so that was one possibility ruled out. Rena's response was backed up by HTR's biographer, Adam Sisman. Sisman told me that the use of the Oughton alias is 'a theory which would be more plausible if there were indeed a Major Oughton on the staff of the 21st Army Group, or whatever it was called by then' – the British Army of the Rhine, as of August 1945.

I told Rena that I'd do some more digging and come back to her. Sadly, I didn't get the chance to do so before she died, but I was spurred on by knowing that

Part One: Rena's Story
Childhood

The 'surplus women' of World War One: Rena's mother (third from right) with her eight sisters.

Rena was an avid reader, from the word 'go'. She also knew, from an early age, that she wanted to work in news.

Teenaged Rena, with her dad, mum and older sister Isobel, on holiday in Glen Lyon.

University

Accessing a whole new world, studying French and German at St Andrews University.

The formidable Professor D'Arcy Wentworth Thompson, Professor of Natural History at St Andrews, from 1917 until his death in 1948. (*Image courtesy of the University of St Andrews Libraries and Museums*)

Rena (third from right) with university friends and her sister (seated, right) – having a (golf) ball!

Bletchley Park

Four firm friends. Clockwise from left: Rena, Margery, Aggie and Elma. (*With permission from the families of Rena, Margery, Elma and Agnes*)

Women made up 75% of the workforce at Bletchley Park. Photo: the Cipher Office, in Block E. (© *Crown Copyright, by kind permission Director GCHQ*)

The building in which Hut 3 was located. (*Author's Own*)

Germany

Rena in post-war Germany. Photo taken in Brunswick (Braunschweig), southeast of Hanover.

Hugh Trevor-Roper, in 1946, when he was elected to a 'Studentship' (Fellowship) at Christ Church College, Oxford. There, he wrote *The Last Days of Hitler*, containing Rena and Margery's translation of Hitler's will. (*Photo provided with permission by the Senior Common Room, Christ Church, Oxford*)

Rena and pals, on parade outside their billet in Bad Nenndorf.

Rena on her 'illegal' trip to Berlin in 1946, pictured outside what she was told was Hitler's bunker.

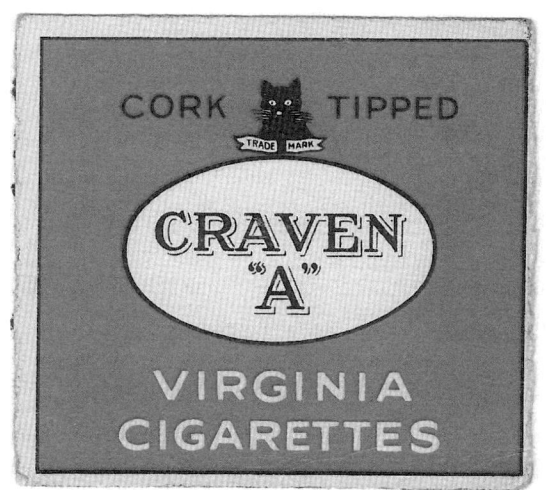 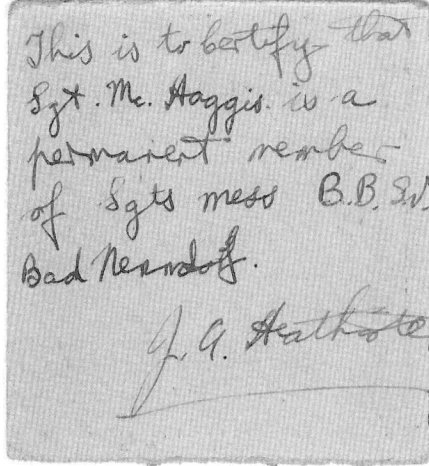

Exhibit 1 from Rena's possessions: a cigarette pack certificate for her alter ego, 'Sgt McHaggis'.

Spring has sprung. Rena in the garden of the house where she was billeted, in April 1946. On the back of the photograph, she wrote 'ain't nature grand!'

The handsome but soon-to-depart Frank.

Out with the girls. Aggie (left) and Rena (second from right).

BBC World Service

No more khaki: Rena, early on in her career at the BBC (April 1948).

Lionel Salter – one of the "very original characters" that Rena worked with at the BBC. Lionel, an English pianist, conductor, writer and administrator (among other things), had a long association with the BBC. (*Courtesy of Lionel's son, Graham Salter*)

Rena worked hard and played hard. On her travels in the former Yugoslavia, looking like a film star. (*Provided by Peter Wesley*)

Rena, loving life as a newsroom journalist (1960s).

Retirement

Rena's retirement book, with touching and humorous comments from her colleagues.

Splendid Scottish dancing: fancy footwork and dashing in and having fun.

VIP visit to the BBC. Painting by the Glasgow gallerist/painter Frances Lowrie, commissioned by Rena's nephew for her 90th birthday, in 2013.

Rena (right) with Catherine (then Duchess of Cambridge) and other veterans, not getting a word in! Bletchley Park, 2019. (*Associated Press/Alamy Stock Photo*)

100th birthday celebrations. Left, with Revd Sue McCoan of St Andrews Church, Ealing, and right, with carer and friend Lidine Winters. (*Photos with permission from Revd and Jamie McCoan*)

Rena, 100 years young, at home in Ealing, in June 2023. (*Author's own*)

Part Two: Remembering Rena's Bletchley Friends

Agnes raises a glass – cheers!
(*Photo provided by Martin Glynn*)

Elma in her later years: still a ray of sunshine. (*Photo provided by Ellie Wasmoeth*)

Smiley Margery in the 1960s.
(*Photo provided by Ed Tarwinski*)

Part Three: Three Mysteries
Mystery One: Bill, Hugh, and Hitler's Wills

Bill and Hugh – a mysterious two! No photo of Bill could be found, but several of HTR – here he is in 1939. (*With permission from the National Archives, Kew (first photo) and Blair Worden (second photo)*)

Dick White (later Sir Dick White), who chose HTR for the vital missions of investigating Hitler's death and wills. (*With permission from Tom Bower*)

Bernd Freytag von Loringhoven – interrogated by Hugh Trevor-Roper about the last days of Hitler. (*Owner of photo unknown*)

The three disappearing messengers. Top photo: Heinz Lorenz (back row, third from left), with Hitler and others, in 1940. Photo held in the German national archive: Bundesarchiv, Bild 183-R99057 / Unbekannt / CC-BY-SA 3.0. (*Johannmeyer: Associated Press / Alamy Stock Photo*)

SS Colonel Wilhelm Zander. (*Photo from ww2gravestone.com*)

Major Willy Johannmeyer. (*Associated Press / Alamy Stock Photo*)

Mystery Two: The Missing Book Room

What the German Book Room might have looked like (photograph of another department – SIXTA). (*Courtesy of the Bletchley Park Trust*)

Block D today – sadly derelict. The central corridor is in the background, with Spur H on the left and Spur I (the nerve centre) to the right. (*Author's own*)

Mystery Three: Missiles and Monitoring

Caversham Park: home of the BBC Monitoring Service from 1943 to 2018. (*Photo by Nick Garrod*)

The Listening Room at Caversham. This photo was taken after the Cuban Missile Crisis, in 1964. However, in 2011, the artist Deborah A. Dismuke used it to create a painting (*Message from Moscow*) which illustrated the key role of Caversham in the crisis. The painting celebrated the 70-year partnership between BBC Monitoring and FBIS/OSE. (© *BBC Archive*)

she wanted to know, as much as I did. I just didn't anticipate what a historical rabbit hole the research would take me down!

As I was digging, I also looked into Rena's own, unresolved question of why Major Oughton asked her and Margery to translate Hitler's personal will, given that other translations, and translators, were already available. So really, Mystery One is two mysteries in one!

The story of Bill, Hugh, and Hitler's wills is relatively long, with many a twist and turn. However, it's intriguing and entertaining, with lots of spy stuff. It also covers events in history with which not many of the general public are familiar with. So, I hope you'll read on!

2

Bill

Returning home from Rena's residence, I resumed my research. I still couldn't find anything about Bill's identity and life *before* Germany but, with some determined googling, I did come across a few clues as to what he seems to have done *afterwards*. I found the first clue (and here comes the first bit of spy stuff!) on the CIA website. The site contained a scanned copy of a book by Nigel West (*The Friends: Britain's Post-War Secret Intelligence Operations*).[1] This mentions a 'Bill Oughton from RAF Fayid' (in northern Egypt), in the 1950s. It also notes that Bill was the head of 'SIME' (Security Intelligence Middle East). The book describes SIME as an 'organisation of Defence Security Officers and Security Liaison Officers' which operated in parallel with SIS (the Secret Intelligence Service – aka MI6).[2] The organisation supported the British Military Government in Egypt with counter and security intelligence. It comprised several British intelligence agencies, with MI5 in the lead. The book goes on to describe SIME as 'Bill Oughton's regional MI5 office at RAF Fayid' and lists him as a future director of MI5.[3] Exciting – it looks like Bill had a stellar career!

The second piece of evidence was a reference to a 'William (Bill) Oughton' on the Wikipedia page about SIME. This confirms that he was head of SIME, between 1953 and 1955.[4] Sometime later, I found a third clue: that *before* SIME, Oughton had worked for its sister organisation 'SIFE' (Security Intelligence Far East).[5] The pieces of the puzzle were a bit jumbled, but they were starting to fall into place.

Surely, I thought, *this must be the same person as Rena's boss: how many majors named Oughton can there have been in British intelligence in 1945/6*? I couldn't be sure about any of it, so I contacted a friend in the Intelligence Corps. She introduced me to Nick Fox (a former Colonel from the Corps, who knows a lot about the Corp's history). Among other things, Colonel Fox was able to answer the question of how many Major Oughtons there could possibly have been. Well, there were at least two! Colonel Fox found another one: a Major *John* Oughton. *This* Major Oughton had started out as a Lance Corporal but progressed quickly to the rank of major. He worked for the Special Operations Executive, whose role was to 'coordinate all action, by way of subversion and sabotage, against the enemy overseas'.[6] However, he doesn't appear to have served at Bad Nenndorf, or in SIFE or SIME, so he can't have been the same person, using a different first name for some reason. But brothers or cousins, perhaps? Who knows!

More importantly, Colonel Fox looked into both *Bill* Oughton's identity/background and HTR and his alias, and then reported back. On Bill Oughton he said:

'There was a William Oughton who was an officer in the Intelligence Corps, but I don't know where he served or whether he reached the rank of Major. The Supplement to the *London Gazette* 26 Nov 1943 shows that: '5829347 C.S.M. [Company Sergeant Major] William Hirst OUGHTON (291292) Suffolk Regt, was granted an immediate Emergency Commission [in the Intelligence Corps] in the rank of 2nd Lieutenant.' Sadly, I cannot link this William Oughton as the person for who Rena was working. He could be one and the same, but he would have had to have advanced very rapidly from 2nd Lieutenant in November '43 to Major in 1945. This is not impossible though; being a former company sergeant major, he would have age, maturity and experience on his side. With reference to the Nigel West book, where he mentions SIME and its Defence Security Officers (DSOs), it is not clear if the William (Bill) Oughton it names as a DSO in SIME (and who later joined MI5) ... is the same person as Rena's boss.'

Two new clues, then: the Suffolk Regiment CSM and the middle or family name Hirst. I contacted the Suffolk Regiment Museum: they had no record of a William or Bill Oughton; nor did the National Archives (where you can apply for access to data on military personnel). Curiouser and curiouser! I'll come back to both clues later.

3

Hugh

Bill was proving tricky to track down, so once again I moved on to HTR and the alias. Could HTR have met Oughton at Bad Nenndorf? Colonel Fox said:

> It is unlikely Major Hugh Trevor-Roper was ever at Bad Nenndorf. He was not involved in interrogating people but was given access, I believe, to some German prisoners of war being held in 'No. 1 War Criminals Holding Centre, Minden', while awaiting their trials, to assist him with his investigation into Hitler's death. Major Hugh Trevor-Roper was attached to SIS [the Secret Intelligence Service, aka MI6], and I expect that he used a pseudonym for such work due to the presence of, and the need to liaise with and exchange documents with, Soviet army officers. These would have included GRU (foreign military intelligence) and NKVD (interior intelligence and security) personnel.[1] No doubt, he was trying to keep his profile and 'footprint' very low. It is difficult to determine if Hugh Trevor-Roper used Major Oughton's name wittingly or unwittingly. A professional intelligence officer would not have used a pseudonym without checking whether there was a real person with the same name; they would not be able to afford the embarrassment of the worst type of coincidences happening! It is possible that Hugh Trevor-Roper might not have been allocated a pseudonym and therefore asked a friend (i.e. Bill) if he could use his as required. Not very professional, but workable.

This was very helpful. The Russian liaison aspect makes sense – although, as I'll explain later, HTR discovered that the Russians were not terribly willing to liaise!

My next move was to consult HTR's best-selling book, *The Last Days of Hitler*, and Adam Sisman's book *Hugh Trevor-Roper, The Biography*.

My first (albeit slightly distracting) thought was that HTR has an *incredible* life story. Someone should make this into a movie, immediately! When *The Last Days of Hitler* was published in 1947, a contact of HTR's had talks with Alfred Hitchcock about a movie based on the book. There were also suggestions of a stage play.[2] For some unknown reason, nothing came of these at the time, although many years later, the movie *Downfall* did dramatise the last days in the bunker. This included the dictator dictating his wills, but not their extraction from the bunker. However, I could imagine a different movie, focused on this young British historian and intelligence officer who (among many other things) investigated Hitler's fate and tracked down his wills. It might well start with HTR in a dark, snowy garden, with a captured German army officer swinging an axe ... about which, see later.

But first, I should provide some background on HTR that explains how he came to write the book which contained Rena and Margery's translation. I find this fascinating – though I have by no means included the whole, movie-worthy story.

When war broke out in 1939, HTR was a young Oxford graduate in Classics and History and a junior research fellow. He would soon (in 1940) become a published author, of a book about an ancient archbishop of Canterbury (Archbishop Laud). He was also a keen huntsman and a Territorial Army cavalry officer (on old-fashioned horseback, not tank). He expected to be called up, but he couldn't have imagined that he would start the war with ... a stint in jail. Well, kind of. In December of that year, HTR was called up for a 'hush-hush' war job with a new secret organisation called the Radio Security Service (RSS). The service had been established in the cells of Wormwood Scrubs Prison in London (the prisoners having been evacuated somewhere safer). This was to be his new office – quite different from the dreaming spires of Oxford! When HTR joined, RSS was part of MI8, the signals intelligence arm of the War Office (which, incidentally, might have recruited Rena), though it later became part of SIS/MI6. The original role of RSS had been to identify illicit wireless signals and radio beacons that Nazi spies in Britain might be using to guide German bombers. However, there wasn't really anything to find, so the service switched to searching for secret messages coming from within Germany.[3]

HTR played a significant role in intelligence throughout the war. Even before it began, he had built up a good understanding of Nazi Germany. He had visited the country in 1935, as a student, hoping to improve his fluency in German, for academic purposes. There, he found himself horrified by life under National Socialism. Just five years later, he and his RSS colleague Walter Gill were fighting the National Socialists, from their prison cell and a shared flat in Ealing. Ealing, coincidentally, is where Rena eventually settled. There, they managed to break a German Abwehr (military intelligence) hand-cipher. Depending on who tells this bit of the story, it was either done over tea and biscuits, and/or while HTR was in the bath during an air raid.[4] It's not clear whether HTR was just sheltering in the tub or actually having a bath (a real eureka moment).

HTR and Gill's breakthrough contributed to many more successes, both by them and by British professional codebreakers who were also working on Abwehr messages.[5] HTR became expert on German secret wireless and on the Abwehr, and he collaborated with Bletchley Park, including with Hut 3.[6] The hand-cipher episode was significant, as it allowed the British to monitor the Abwehr more effectively, which HTR believed contributed to the cracking of the Enigma code.[7] He wasn't universally liked in the intelligence world (some thought him a maverick and disrespectful of territory). In return, he was critical of some of his colleagues. This meant that his efforts were not always appreciated. Regardless, he seems to have been an effective intelligence officer.

By the end of the war, HTR was working in the Allies' Counter-Intelligence War Room in London. He had some final assignments to complete and was due to take up a research lectureship in History at Christ Church College, Oxford. Perhaps he was looking forward to studying more ancient archbishops – that is, until he was selected for a special mission: to find out what had happened to Hitler. Although Hitler had (it would later be confirmed) committed suicide and had his body burned, there were rumours swirling that he had escaped. As Rena mentioned, this was worrying. There were genuine fears at the time that there would be a Nazi revival.

The Russians had been the first of the Allies to enter Hitler's bunker and were therefore most likely among the victors to know the truth. Brigadier Dick White (head of counterintelligence in the British Zone) had discussed the matter with Marshal Zhukov (Soviet commander in Germany) sometime previously to HTR's involvement. Zhukov had confirmed that Hitler had killed himself and had his body burned. To prove this, he had shown White a set of false teeth identified as Hitler's![8] These, and a piece of his jawbone, were all that could be recovered from the ashes.[9]

A few days later, however, the Russians had changed their story. They now denied that they had found his body after all, speculated that he could have escaped, and refused to make any further comment. This about-turn seems to have come from Stalin himself, who later told the same story to President Truman's envoy, Harry Hopkins.[10] Rumours and Soviet media stories followed. For example, there were claims that Hitler had fled to Dublin and disguised himself as a woman, or to Argentina by submarine.[11] These rumours opened up the possibility that Hitler might return, and perhaps with force.

This story might be what Rena confused into a recollection of the Russians finding Hitler's *wills* in the bunker and concealing them. Instead, it was all to do with his fate/body. In any case, even if the wills *had* been there, it seems unlikely that the Russian soldiers who entered the bunker would have had the wherewithal to have taken them: Adam Sisman reports that they took Hitler's hairbrush as a trophy but left his engagement diary.[12]

The British thought it vital to investigate Hitler's fate; to establish the facts and prevent a myth from developing. In particular, they needed to prevent any claims that he had died a heroic death. What finally secured approval for the investigation was more game-playing by the Russians, who eventually accused the British of *hiding* Hitler and his wife.[13] Although they were allies, even at this early stage they were not all exactly the best of friends.

Brigadier White would commission the investigation, and he needed the right person to lead it. He already knew HTR, respected his analysis of German Intelligence and considered him a 'first-rate chap'. HTR visited White in a requisitioned castle near Bad Oeynhausen, in September 1945. While there, he gave White an account (over three bottles of hock!) of what was known so far about Hitler's fate. This account convinced White that HTR was 'the chap who ... [had] kept the closest tabs on the matter' and hence the man for the job. He offered it to him there and then, and HTR accepted gladly.[14] This must have been a dream job for a historian.

HTR returned home, but he travelled back out to Germany that same month to conduct his investigation into Hitler's fate. By coincidence, September was also when Rena made her 'epic' journey across battle-scarred Europe. The only difference was that HTR got to go by plane instead of by decrepit train! It was an urgent and important job, after all, and he had no time to waste. There were piles of documentation to sift through and a list of potential witnesses to interrogate or have interrogated. He would make several visits to Hitler's bunker, now flooded with water. He would also need to liaise with the British, Americans and Russians. However, the Russians, who had some key witnesses in custody, would not oblige. Understandably, perhaps, HTR dismissed them as: 'those incompetent and obstructive barbarians of the East'![15] It wasn't all serious, though: he reported rather enjoying driving all over Germany on his mission. He wrote of 'delightful journeys' through 'deciduous golden groves', visiting the 'great Danish castle of Ploen', and watching wild duck on their last flight before sunset.[16]

HTR's biography confirms that he conducted his investigation 'using the cover name Major Oughton'.[17] But did he know him? I think he *must* have. If Rena recalled that they were friends, that's proof enough for me. He might have known him for years; or perhaps only from visits to Bad Oeynhausen on War Room business, if Oughton were visiting too. However, I still wasn't certain, at this point in my research, whether HTR ever went to Bad *Nenndorf,* where Rena and Margery worked. This was located approximately 50km away.

I think I managed to solve the Bad Nenndorf question, as it happens. The alias 'Major Oughton' also appears in a book called *In the Bunker with Hitler: The Last Witness Speaks*, by Bernd Freytag von Loringhoven. Von Loringhoven was a German officer who was present in the bunker with Hitler, and responsible for preparing reports for him. In his book, von Loringhoven wrote that, as a prisoner after the war, he was flown to Bad Nenndorf. There, he recalled a Major Oughton, as 'the man employed to interrogate me ... most of the time ... to do with the last days in the bunker'. But was this the *real* Major Oughton, or HTR using his alias? My guess is it was the latter. Why? It's unlikely that HTR would miss the opportunity to interview this key witness from a small pool (asking 'very detailed questions for hours on end'). In the book, von Loringhoven added: 'I discovered subsequently that Major Oughton was the assumed name of Hugh Trevor-Roper, a member of the British secret service and a future Oxford professor, author of an acclaimed book published shortly after the war.'

Incidentally, von Loringhoven did mention that HTR showed him a kindness one day. He reported to HTR that he was suffering very poor treatment by 'highly aggressive guard[s]' at the camp. HTR (perhaps via Major Oughton, or even 'Tin Eye' Stephens) saw to it that this stopped.[18] Anyway, neither von Loringhoven nor Sisman's book explains why HTR chose that name nor mentions a real-life Bill Oughton. Sisman doesn't know, and I presume that von Loringhoven didn't, either.

The intelligence historian E.D.R. Harrison, a friend of Sisman's who has written about HTR, is also aware of the mystery around the alias. He told me: 'Trevor-Roper's investigation was *military* intelligence rather than secret service, and he was never a slave of official secrecy. Initially, at least, he needed awareness of his mission in Allied military circles, and knowledge of his identity would help witnesses if they needed to contact him again. Perhaps after some weeks he felt knowledge of his mission was getting out of hand, and that by using 'Oughton' he could have some concealment, but that information sent to the real Major Oughton would eventually reach him anyway. But this is speculative.' This seems plausible and pragmatic.

HTR concluded his investigation in October and reported his findings to the Allies' Quadripartite Intelligence Committee (of Britain, the USA, France and Russia). Among other details, he confirmed that Hitler and Eva Braun had committed suicide in the bunker and that Hitler had shot himself. Until then, it was thought that he had used poison, like Braun.[19] He also confirmed that their bodies had been burnt, as Hitler had requested. A secondary benefit of the report was that it allowed HTR to show up the 'incompetent and obstructive barbarians of the East'. It was the Russians that had originally claimed that Hitler had chosen a coward's death, by poison. Now, they had to admit that

that was not correct. When asked questions about the remaining witnesses and the body, their answer was very short (and you must read this with your best Russian accent): 'very interesting'.[20]

HTR knew that there were still some gaps in the story (which he and others would continue to work on). The British, Americans and French still hadn't seen Hitler's body (or at least the rest of it), so rumours persisted. Meanwhile, the Russians still had key witnesses in captivity, and Martin Bormann (Hitler's personal secretary) was still missing. Bormann had, in fact, died trying to escape Berlin, but his remains were not discovered until over 60 years later.[21] Hitler was finally issued a death certificate in 1956, after the witnesses in Russian captivity had been released and could give evidence.[22] This evidence (along with documentation which surfaced much later, after the fall of Communism) confirmed HTR's findings. However, in November 1945 his findings were judged to be confirmation enough. They were also helpful for the smooth conduct of the Nuremberg Trials, which were about to start.[23] And so, once he had delivered his report (*The Last Days of Hitler and Eva Brown*) and briefed the media, on 1 November, HTR's job was done. He flew back to England to get on with the important business of being a historian (or a more normal one, at least).[24]

4
Hitler's Wills

But then came the matter of Hitler's wills – so I *am* coming back to Rena and Margery; just via the scenic route! HTR had not long been back in England when he received a phone call from Bad Oeynhausen, saying that a document had been found that 'purported to be Hitler's will'.[1] HTR was already aware that there were three sets of the wills. Goebbels had mentioned their existence in a telegram to Grand Admiral Karl Dönitz (head of the Navy and then President), which was found at the end of the war. Thus, HTR knew that there were two more sets to be found. Dönitz had been a committed follower of Hitler and had wished to continue the war. Hitler had chosen the Admiral to succeed him as head of state because he trusted no one else. The new president had sprung into action and set up government, at the naval academy in Flensburg, near Denmark.[2] However, his period in office was to be very short: appointed on 30 April, he surrendered on 7 May and dissolved the government on 23 May 1945.

After his investigation into Hitler's fate, HTR was the perfect candidate to look into the matter of the wills. I'll come back to this second mission shortly, but firstly I'll explain what happened to the documents, up until the point at which HTR received his phone call.

As mentioned, the wills had not been left in the bunker, as Rena believed. Instead, Hitler had arranged for them to be given to three messengers, each of whom had a different intended recipient or destination. The messengers and their missions were as follows:[3]

- **Heinz Lorenz**
    - Job title: **Hitler's Deputy Chief Press Secretary.**
    - Documents carried: **Hitler's original political testament and personal will**, along with Goebbels' *Appendix to the Führer's Political Testament*. In the appendix, Goebbels stated that he had chosen to ignore Hitler's order to escape to Berlin and join the new government. Instead, he, his wife and six small children would stay and die in the bunker with Hitler.[4] The poor children would be poisoned with cyanide.
    - Mission: Take the documents to the **headquarters of Admiral Dönitz** in Flensburg, or elsewhere in British or American territory. Ensure

that the documents would eventually be kept in the Party archives in **Munich**, the home of the Nazi movement. Bormann selected Lorenz for this mission, as 'a young man with plenty of initiative', and with 'a good chance of getting through'.[5]

- **SS Colonel Wilhelm Zander**
  - Job title: **Personal adviser to Martin Bormann**
  - Documents carried: **Copies of the wills**, along with the **marriage certificate** of Hitler and Eva Braun, and a **note from Bormann**.
  - Mission: Deliver to **Admiral Dönitz** himself (in Flensburg).
- **Major Willy Johannmeyer**
  - Job title: **Hitler's army adjutant**
  - Documents carried: **A copy of the political testament** and a **cover letter by General Wilhelm Burgdorf** (Hitler's chief adjutant).
  - Mission: Get his documents out of Berlin, at any price, and deliver them to **Field Marshal Ferdinand Schörner** (the new Commander-in-Chief of the Army) in Czechoslovakia. Escort the other messengers.

Hitler dispatched the three men, together with a corporal named Hummerich, at noon on 29 April. This was the day before his suicide. They were heading West – likely because they thought that they'd have a better chance in American territory than in an area held by the Russians. There was widespread and justified fear of the Red Army. Still, this didn't ensure that it would be an easy, quick or successful mission. Even getting out of Berlin was a huge challenge: the city was under bombardment by the Russians, and they had to pass through three Russian lines. They survived, and then rested until nightfall with a battalion of Hitler Youth. These were teenaged boys, tasked with defending a key bridge over the River Havel from the Red Army, and with facilitating the escape of figures from the regime. Sadly, fewer than 500 of the 4.5–5,000 boys survived the assault.[6]

The messengers then hit the road again – or rather, the river. They took two boats and started making their way down the River Havel, which flows past Berlin and away to the West. Johannmeyer, in one boat, reached the German-held bridgehead at Wannsee and radioed Dönitz for a plane.[7] The group then reconvened, and sailed to a river island called Pfaueninsel, to await the plane's arrival.[8] However, the Russians started bombing the island, so they were forced to flee. They requisitioned a canoe, paddled away and took shelter in a yacht that was moored nearby. The plane (a seaplane) did eventually arrive, but at the vital moment it all went horribly wrong (from their perspective, at least). By this time, the four had split into separate boats again, with Johannmeyer still on the yacht. Zander and Lorenz reached the seaplane, but Zander's boat was shaken, and the others got distracted trying to rescue him. In the meantime, the Russians attacked the plane, forcing it to fly off without them. 'By such a narrow margin,' HTR remarked, 'did Johannmeier and his companions fail in their mission.'[9]

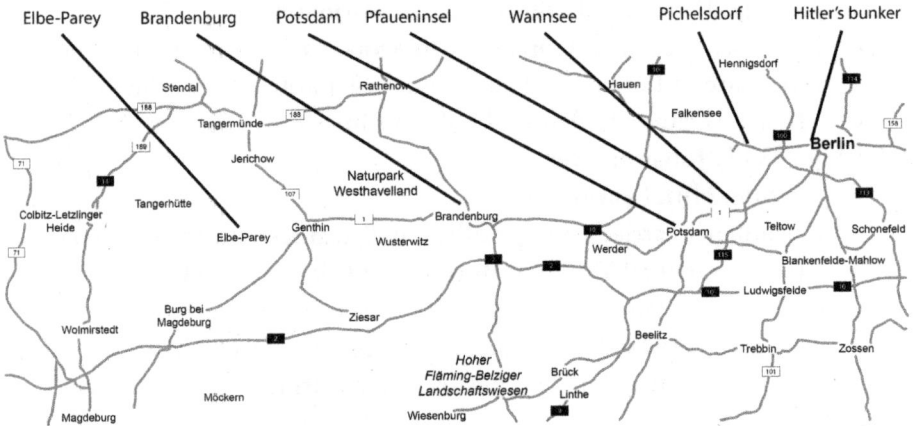

Figure 2: The bunker and beyond: the route taken by Johannmeier, Lorenz, Zander and Hummerich, from East to West, on their failed mission.

Not deterred, the fugitives continued their wingless flight westwards, via Potsdam and Brandenburg. By 11 May (12 days in), they were over 100km from Hitler's bunker but still not home and dry. They crossed the River Elbe at Parey, disguised themselves as foreign workers and sneaked into the area of the Western Allies in American trucks. They then heard that Admiral Dönitz had surrendered, and that the war was over. At this news, they decided to abandon their missions and disappear, although Johannmeier still believed that he could have completed his mission. They split up – I shall take the liberty of assuming that this was with a last but pointless 'Heil Hitler' – and went their own ways.

A few months later, Lorenz was almost captured. He had fled to Luxembourg, adopted the alias 'Georges Thiers' and become a journalist – a logical move, as an ex-Deputy Chief Press Secretary. That summer, he approached the British military government in Hanover, seeking employment and offering valuable inside information about life in the bunker. 'Georges' was unable to explain how he was in the know, so the British declined his application.

They got him in the end, but only by chance. In November 1945, Lorenz was arrested for the rather unexciting crime of carrying false identity papers. At that time, he admitted his real name but no more.[10] He was sent to Fallingbostel prison camp, north of Hanover, arriving in the middle of the night. There, a soldier happened to manhandle him because he was moving along too slowly. In doing so, the soldier noticed that the prisoner's coat had unusually bulky shoulder pads. He inspected these and found the documents, sewn into the coat's lining. Lorenz was interrogated and revealed the whole story, which matched the November press release. He confirmed the existence of the copies of the wills and the marriage certificate. He also gave up Johannmeyer and Zander's names and descriptions. The British believed his account, and the documents, to be authentic, having consulted a handwriting expert to check Hitler's signature.[11] One down; two to go.

This was also the point at which the documents were first translated (pre-Rena and Margery). At 5 a.m. in the camp at Fallingbostel, a Captain John Rollo Reid of the British Intelligence Corps gathered a group of five German-born, Jewish, bilingual British soldiers into a room.[12] He locked the door and tasked them with carrying out this important, top-secret job. When the job was done, Reid took four men and all the documents to Lieutenant General Brian Horrocks of the British Army's 'XXX Corps'.[13] Horrocks announced to the men that he would be phoning London with the good news, and then he popped a bottle of champagne.[14] I'd like to think that he did this with a jolly 'Cheers, chaps!'

5

The Investigation

Somewhere in Christ Church College, Oxford, a phone rang. It was mid-December 1945, and Bad Oeynhausen were calling HTR to offer him a new mission (should he choose to accept). This time he was to track down Johannmeyer and Zander, and thereby to find and authenticate the whole set of wills. And so, his academic aspirations interrupted one last time, Hugh flew straight back out to Germany.

HTR had no prior knowledge of Zander, but he did know of Johannmeyer, and he managed to locate him quickly, on 20 December. Like Lorenz, Johannmeyer was apparently not very good at hiding (!): he was living with his parents, in the city of Iserlohn, near Dortmund. Johannmeyer was taken off to be interrogated. Incidentally, his interrogator was a young Czech Jewish officer named Ján Hoch, who later became the famous media mogul Robert Maxwell. Hoch's attempts to extract the truth were unsuccessful, so HTR took over. Johannmeyer did then admit that he had been in Hitler's bunker, but he didn't (or wouldn't) say any more. Instead, he claimed that he was merely a simple soldier who had escorted Lorenz and Zander through Russian lines but had no knowledge of what the documents were. HTR knew that Johannmeyer was a seasoned veteran who had served on the Eastern Front, and he just didn't believe him. Therefore, he ordered that Johannmeyer be kept in custody over Christmas, in solitary confinement, while he focused on the hunt for Zander.[1]

Also on the hunt was an American: Agent Arnold H. Weiss from the US Counter Intelligence Corps (CIC). Weiss hoped to find Zander too, but in *his* case, this was as a stepping stone to finding Martin Bormann. A list of major war criminals was being prepared, in hopes of prosecuting them. At this point, the list included Hitler and Bormann, as their fates weren't known. Weiss had worked out that Zander hailed from Munich, which was a good start. He notified British intelligence, and HTR was brought on board, on around 20/21 December.[2] For his part, HTR told the Americans that Zander had the papers in his possession.

HTR set himself up in the headquarters of the American Commander-in-Chief. He then headed off to search Zander's flat, in Munich, but he found nothing. It was Christmas Eve, and he must have felt quite frustrated. However, pure chance then intervened again. He returned to American HQ briefly, to pack up his belongings. As he was doing so, two passing Americans glanced at his papers and exclaimed: 'Zander again!'[3] When he pressed them, one of the soldiers revealed that 'the German girlfriend of a friend of his had once been the closest friend of Frau Zander. But that there had been a bitter quarrel, and now the girl would tell anything she knew to sweeten her revenge.' The British interrogated Frau Zander, who told copious, convincing lies about the fugitive.[4]

Strangely, *The Last Days of Hitler* doesn't mention Weiss. Perhaps that reflects a certain amount of disdain that HTR had for the Americans, as I'll explain later on, or perhaps he just wanted all the glory to himself! Another (American) report, on the US National Archives-linked website *The Text Message*, describes Weiss's role in detail. For example, it says that he detained Zander's mother and sister, who did mention a girlfriend.[5] The girlfriend (possibly the same revenge-seeker that HTR had heard of) told the Americans that Zander had assumed an alias: Friedrich-Wilhelm Paustin. He was working as a market gardener in the town of Tegernsee, about 50km south of Munich. What a career change, from personal adviser to one of the top Nazis! Weiss also received information that Zander had applied for a residence permit in the village of Vilshofen, not far from the Austrian border. This information was correlated with military hospital records (Zander had spent time in a military hospital), which included an address in Tegernsee.[6] The net was closing in.

HTR set out for Tegernsee (with Weiss, if you read the American account) and raided Zander's new home there, but again, he and his documents were nowhere to be found. HTR discovered that Zander had gone away to spend

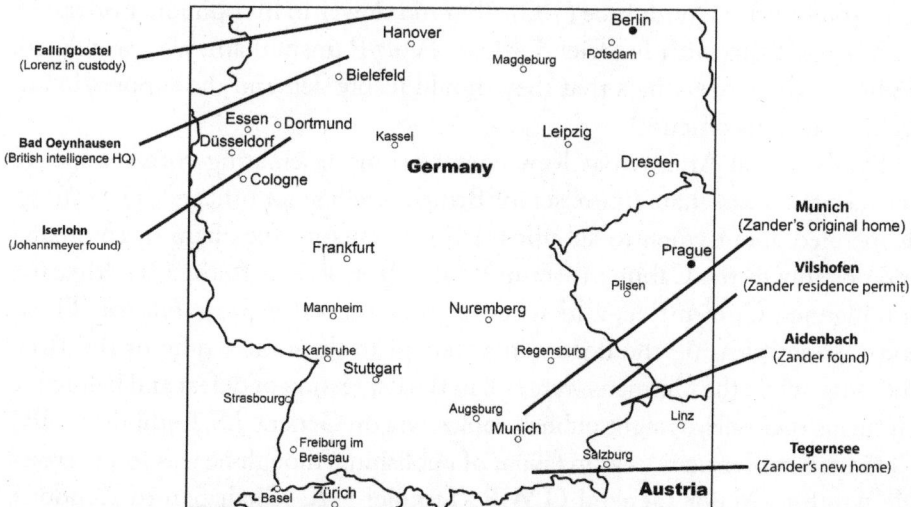

Figure 3: Bad will hunting: some of the main locations in the hunt. A lot of driving for HTR!

Christmas in the village of Aidenbach, near Vilshofen, with a woman called Ilsa Unterholzner. Unterholzner had been one of Bormann's secretaries. Now, perhaps there was a perfectly innocent explanation for this, but it's not clear if Zander's wife, who was very loyal but had already been cheated on at least once, was aware of this arrangement!

On the night of 28 December, HTR (and Weiss?!) set out for Aidenbach in an American jeep. It was to be a long drive, in treacherous conditions, and 3am by the time they arrived at the farmhouse where Zander was thought to be staying. HTR stationed an armed man at each corner of the house and knocked on the door. There was no answer. He then instructed a German policeman to enter through a window. Once inside, he entered a bedroom and saw 'a giant nose, the unmistakeable nose of Bormann's assistant, SS Standartenfuehrer [Colonel] Wilhelm Zander.'[7] The nose was attached to Zander himself, who was in *bed* with Unterholzner (no innocent explanation, then)!

Initially, Zander insisted that he was Wilhelm Paustin, but he was dragged out of bed, arrested and taken for interrogation. He then admitted his true identity. He also confessed that he had hidden his set of the documents in a suitcase in Tegernsee while he was away for Christmas. The reason HTR hadn't found this at Zander's home is that he had hidden the case at the home of Unterholzner's sister-in-law, *Irmgard* Unterholzner. As it happened, Irmgard was not as loyal to the cause as Ilsa: she had already reported the suitcase to the authorities.

So, mission *almost* accomplished – but could it be announced already? HTR believed that the existence of the wills should be made public, but that the British military leadership were too nervous about doing so. Information relating to the wills had been percolating upwards to the British decision-makers – the Joint Intelligence Committee (JIC) – but too slowly, in his opinion. Frustrated, he discussed this with his friend, Major Peter Ramsbotham, who wondered: 'Who are these brass-hats that they should feebly demand the suppression of an historical document?'[8]

The National Archives at Kew contain some fascinating correspondence between the 'brass-hats' (more senior British intelligence officers). The officers deliberated about when to submit the documents up the chain of command and possibly to the Cabinet (over in England), as well as to the Quadripartite Intelligence Committee, and whether to send out a press release. Those considering releasing the documents wanted to do so at a time of the Brits' choosing, while the Germans were still in the depression of defeat and before the Germans themselves might publish copies. Major-General J.S. Lethbridge (JIC Chairman in Germany) was in favour of publishing, though he was still nervous. He wrote to Major General G.W.R. Templer (JIC Chairman in London): 'My dear Tubby! ... I feel it in my blood that [releasing the documents] may have political repercussions'.⁹ He judged that the prosaic personal will showed Hitler in a 'not unfavourable light', which must have worried him.¹⁰ In addition, Lethbridge didn't want the news to leak to 'the yellow Press' (American tabloid newspapers); he felt that it should be a British 'scoop'. He adds a PS, however: 'My own advice is to buy shares in some 'yellow' newspaper and then sell for a copyright, and then retire.'¹¹

Even before finding Zander, the rebellious HTR had decided to report straight away to the Americans, should he find the documents. That said, Zander *was* found within the American occupation zone, so there was some sense, and perhaps a duty, to do so. Once in possession of the documents, American military intelligence did their own translation of the documents (again, pre-Rena and Margery). HTR secured an agreement with the Americans that the documents should remain top secret for the time being.¹²

And yet, all was still not well with the Allies. The intelligence historian E.D.R. Harrison explains in an essay that, just one day later, HTR was handed an American military newspaper (*Stars and Stripes*) which celebrated the find as an *American* success, with no mention of British involvement.¹³ All the deliberations of the brass-hats had been in vain. 'Events,' Colonel L.H.F. Sanderson of the Intelligence Corps remarked, had 'forestalled a decision on this matter'.¹⁴ General Truscott, Commander of the United States Third Army, appeared to have 'let the cat out of the bag on his own responsibility'.¹⁵

In response, HTR called his own press conference at British HQ and provided some (still limited) information about the wills. In a strange twist, Truscott (and a Colonel Sands of US intelligence) went on to accuse HTR of spiriting documents out of the American Zone (in other words, stealing them).¹⁶ It's fair to say that it wasn't just the *Russians* that HTR wasn't too keen on! Meanwhile, the JIC in London was not pleased with HTR either, for being 'unable to prevent premature release' of the documents.¹⁷

Still, only two of the three sets of documents had been found, so far. HTR returned to Johannmeyer in jail on 1 January 1946. He informed him of the developments and told him that he simply didn't believe his version of events. Johannmeyer continued to deny all knowledge, almost persuading HTR. However, after being left alone for two hours while HTR attended to some other business, he finally admitted: 'Ich habe die Papiere' (I have the papers). Johannmeyer had had time to reflect and had concluded that he was disappointed by how easily the two others (far more senior figures than he, and Nazi Party officials) had given in. To retrieve the papers, they would need to go to his family home in Iserlohn.¹⁸

And this is where the axe came into it (thankfully safely), on a dark, snowy night in early January 1946. HTR and Johannmeyer travelled some distance to Iserlohn. They left HTR's British staff car a way off, so as not to be noticed by disapproving neighbours, and they walked to the house. HTR was alone, in the dark, with Johannmeyer, when Johannmeyer picked up an axe. This must briefly have concerned HTR, but the soldier went into the garden and used it first to break the frozen ground and then to crack open a bottle that he'd buried there. Inside were the documents.[19] Finally, it was mission accomplished: the authenticity of the wills could now be confirmed.

6
The Book

HTR returned to England in January 1946 to start his new job at the University of Oxford. At the suggestion of Dick White, he would also start writing *The Last Days of Hitler* (originally called *Hitler's End*), which featured Rena and Margery's translation. The investigation had had an important purpose; so did the book. HTR explained: 'Hitler's reign was so evil, his character so detestable, that no one can be seduced into admiring him by reading the true history either of his life or of his melodramatic and carefully stage-managed end.'[1]

7

The Translation

And so, after that interesting detour all over Germany, let's get back to Rena and Margery, at that point in time busy typing up statements at Bad Nenndorf. It was also in January 1946 that our two translators' day-to-day duties were livened up considerably, by being assigned their top-secret task.

I haven't been able to confirm *indisputably* why Rena and Margery were selected to do the translation, when other translations (and translators) were already available. The work was requested in January 1946, so was it intended specifically for *The Last Days of Hitler*? Rena had a theory: that HTR might have outsourced the translation like this (rather than do it himself or ask one of the staff at Bad Oeynhausen) because he was working on his book on what should have been army time. She thought that he might not have wanted people to know that he was doing so! A good guess, but HTR had already left the Army and was back in Oxford when Dick White proposed the idea of the book. He didn't start writing it until February.

Alternative possibilities include that: 1) HTR dropped in on Oughton at some point *before* he left Germany and asked him for the translation to be done, as part of his onward study into Hitler's fate. It might then just have been fortuitous that it was also available for inclusion in the book, once the book was proposed; 2) HTR phoned Oughton, from Oxford; or 3) Rena misremembered, and it was actually in *February* that she and Margery were given their top-secret task.

In any scenario, I wondered whether having the translation done *properly/officially* (by Intelligence Corps translators under his trusted friend, Major Oughton) was important to him. In HTR's biography, Adam Sisman writes: 'Since Hugh had gathered much of his source material in an official inquiry, any book arising out of this would need official approval ... by the Joint Intelligence Committee.'[1] And HTR himself stated that he wrote the book 'with the permission and support of the British Intelligence authorities.'[2] I wondered if HTR also felt that he needed to keep the Committee happy because of his reputation for not always toeing the line, and possibly for having taken the results of his investigation to the Americans first.

Knowing his topic so well, HTR wrote *The Last Days of Hitler* quickly. However, its publication was delayed, as he had promised not to release it until the conclusion of the Nuremberg Trials. In fact, he attended the trials, in order to obtain final pieces of evidence for the book.[3] The trials ended in October 1946, two months before Rena and Margery were demobbed and went home. Rena would not necessarily have known, but the trials would have been the reason that she could only divulge that she had been involved in the translation in March 1947, when the book was published.

The New Statesman described *The Last Days of Hitler* as 'a triumph of scientific investigation'. A small part of that triumph – all the careful translation – can, I believe, be attributed to Rena and Margery. And, if *HTR, The Movie* is ever made, there *must* be a scene where our two heroines are portrayed by beautiful, glamorous actresses, studiously translating Hitler's will. Some unknown person has already created a page for Rena on IMDb, the entertainment information and rating site (as if she were a famous actress), so it's got to happen![4]

8

… and Back to Bill

But finally, WHO WAS BILL OUGHTON? Like a good spy, he continued to elude me! I'm no historian or detective, but I certainly tried my best to find out. I even contacted MI5 (a bit nervously), shortly before Rena died. I wanted to see if they had a historian who might be able to help. There was no response, but I thought, with a smile, *they must be busy – 'MI5 not 9 to 5'!*[1] As mentioned, I was hoping to solve the mystery before Rena died, so that I could report back to her, but sadly that wasn't possible.

Having gone down the HTR historical rabbit hole and found so much, I was frustrated that I still knew so little about his friend Bill. In particular, there was still nothing at all concrete about his life before Bad Nenndorf. The Suffolk Regiment CSM might have been a red herring, but I persevered. I tried again to find out more about our man possibly-in-MI5; this time with a new tactic. I simply typed 'MI5' into LinkedIn (as you do!) to see if there was any one at least *connected* to it that I could discover. This led me to a friend of a friend, Robert Hutton, a journalist and author with an interest in history and secret intelligence. Robert told me that there is a Bill Oughton who appears in the diaries of Guy Liddell, the former Deputy Head of MI5, quite frequently, from January 1948 onwards.[2] So I had a look, and I'm very glad I did!

The diaries reveal that, for some time after the war, a Bill Oughton worked as an officer for MI5. There, he collaborated with the police in the UK to counter the rise of Communism, for example in industry. Bill also gave evidence for the trial of Colonel 'Tin Eye' Stephens, in relation to the Colonel's conduct at Bad Nenndorf.[3] This proves that he was Rena's boss (tick)! The diaries confirm that he served in SIFE and SIME. Hutton said: 'The final reference is to him is a W.H. Oughton, so it seems like he might be your man.' I presumed that the 'H' was Hirst. Hutton added that this reference was to Oughton's promotion to become a senior officer in MI5. I'm not familiar with the structure of the organisation, but it seemed plausible to me that he could indeed have gone on to be a director too (if those are two different ranks).

And then, just as I was about to close my investigation, unfinished, an email dropped into my inbox from … MI5! The very pleasant, unnamed person – whom I'll call Bob – mentioned that he (or she?) had heard about Rena's death.

I think Rena would have been delighted at receiving condolences from MI5! Bob also explained MI5's policy, which is that they do not disclose the identities of those that they have employed in the last 50 years, whether they are alive or deceased. But, since Bill was employed over 50 years ago *and* deceased, s/he was able to help. Hooray! And Bob said that MI5 did indeed have a record of our Bill. Some of this I'd already found out, but there were new bits too. In a nutshell, and slightly paraphrased:

> William (known as Bill) Hirst Oughton was born on 14 January 1916, in Wombwell, Yorkshire. He served in the military from 1939 until September 1946 and worked at Bad Nenndorf, Germany, from August 1945 until September 1946, serving as an officer in the Intelligence Corps. He joined MI5 in December 1946. He served in Security Intelligence Far East (SIFE), based in Singapore, from September 1950 to 1952, when he transferred to Security Intelligence Middle East (SIME). Mr Oughton was H/SIME [head of SIME] from December 1953 until December 1954 (presumably based in Cairo) then moved to Cyprus, returning to London in late 1955. He served as acting director in charge of E Branch (then responsible for Counter-Subversion) for a short period. He left MI5 in 1958 due to ill health and passed away in 1976.

What did Bill do between 1916 and 1939, and was he related to Major *John* Oughton? What part of the Army did he join originally, and was this as a soldier or officer? Could he have gone south and joined the Suffolk Regiment? Why not join a regiment closer to home? Could the family have moved? Could he really have risen from Private in 1939 to CSM in 1943 and Major by 1945? What did he look like? So many questions; not many answers, and no photos. Perhaps someone from his family will read this and get in touch.

The very last thing was that the details 14 January 1916 and Wombwell, Yorkshire, were important, and possibly the key to identifying Bill fully. I went online, found the Wombwell Facebook group and requested help. The good people of this small town (which happens to be about 10 minutes' drive from my publisher's office in Barnsley) were very keen to assist. They shared the post and asked around. It turns out that there are some Oughtons in the area, but unfortunately, they aren't related to Bill. So perhaps the family *did* move away.

I wended my way online, via the local vicar, through to the City of Doncaster Archives, which hold old parish records for Wombwell. A representative from the Archives told me that there was a record of a William Hirst Oughton, son of Harry (a colliery official) and Margaret, of Windmill Road. She revealed that his date of birth was 14 *August* 1916 (not January), and that he was baptised on

10 September that year. I did write to the current residents of the Oughtons' previous address, but there was no reply, and to the nearby Wombwell Main Cricket Club (because I thought that perhaps he was a member), but there was no record of him. An archivist then let me know that, according to the census of 1921 (when Bill was 4), the family moved to a village just north of Warrington. Sadly, I couldn't find the house, and there, the trail ran cold. I thought I'd dug enough, and in any case, I had a book to finish!

This has been a long and complicated mystery (the next ones are shorter, don't worry). You might well be asking, why go to all this effort – why does this matter? Well, in my view, Rena mattered, and so do all her wartime colleagues. I'd like to record them for posterity and recognise their service. Second World War history is like a huge jigsaw. I think we'll be adding pieces to it for ever, but we won't ever quite finish it, nor ever bore of it. In any case, I think Rena would have been particularly interested and entertained by this mystery. I hope you have been, too!

Mystery Two

The Missing German Book Room

1

The Mystery

How can a room go missing? In the secret, busy world of Bletchley Park, quite easily! Finding it? Less so.

The second mystery also arose while I was working on the first draft of Rena's story. I looked up the German Book Room online and, as with Bill Oughton, I could hardly find a thing. There were only a few mentions in the small number of articles relating to Rena and her friends. Even on my first research visit to the museum at Bletchley Park, I struggled to learn much more. I asked a couple of room/hut guides about GBR. They hadn't heard of it but were – like me – interested to find out.

Rena had told me that 'GBR came **under Hut 3**' (meaning organisationally), but I realised on my visit that this was not the Hut 3 that you can go into at the museum today. Its *name* is also deceptive: Rena's 'hut' wasn't a hut at all! At the beginning of the war, the original Hut 3 was established in a small building near the mansion and then moved to a second building, not far away. This is the one that you can visit. However, when the codebreakers succeeded in cracking Enigma, the level of activity and the number of staff at the Park increased significantly. The expansion led to the work of this 'illustrious molehill' being moved again; this time to much larger and definitely not hut-like premises.[1] It was business time at Bletchley!

For the period of the war when Rena was working at the Park, Hut 3 was housed in a purpose-built office complex called 'Block D'. It shared the complex with two other departments: Huts 6 and 8. Block D is now a Grade II listed building, and historians have studied it in detail, but even *they* haven't managed to work out exactly where GBR was located within it. No photos of the room itself survive that could help to do this. You can't just go in and have a look, either, because the building is now derelict and hence closed to the public.[2] Nevertheless, since GBR was the workplace of not just Rena but also 40-plus other women, *and* since it has its own song, I decided to try to solve the small mystery of its location.

At my disposal I had Rena's own testimony and a Historic Buildings Report on Bletchley Park, produced by English Heritage in 2004.[3] The report contains several site plans of Block D, including those shown opposite, in Figure 4. Frustratingly, I only came across the report after Rena had died – otherwise I could have just whipped it out and asked her to point to GBR on one of the plans. But that would have been too easy, and I wouldn't have had all the fun of looking into it! So, with Rena resting in peace, I got sleuthing.

2
The Investigation

My first task was to *understand* Block D. This was easier said than done, because of the complicated work that was done in there, and because the building evolved over time. Block D was a single-storey 'spider block' – a building with a central corridor, and 'spurs' of offices protruding at right angles on either side. There were 13 spurs altogether, lettered A to M. The new Hut 3 essentially occupied the left-hand side of the building (Spurs A, B, C, G, H and I) and the central corridor between these. However, in the diagram below, Spur C is not included in Hut 3. This is because it was occupied, at the time the site plan was drawn up, by '6IS' (6 Intelligence School). This was a unit that analysed radio traffic patterns (as opposed to breaking codes and reading messages). 6IS moved to Block G, just north of Block D, in late 1943, and Rena arrived in early 1944.

The report includes a study of the huts in Block D, and each of the rooms within, as they were in 1943. The authors tried to identify the purpose of each

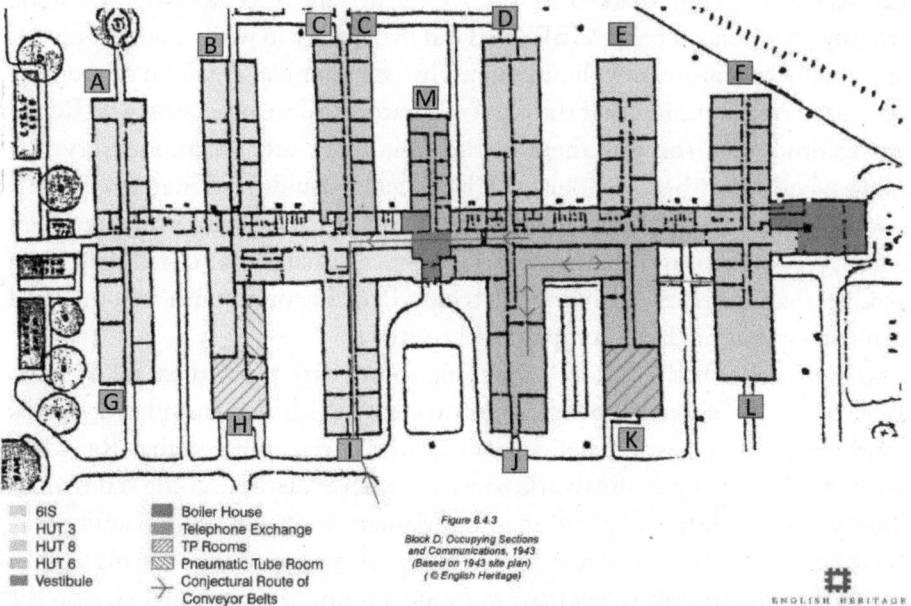

Figure 4: Block D site plan, from 1943, showing the location of Hut 3. Spur letters added by the author. Image from a 2004 English Heritage Historic Building Report on Bletchley Park. (© *Historic England*)

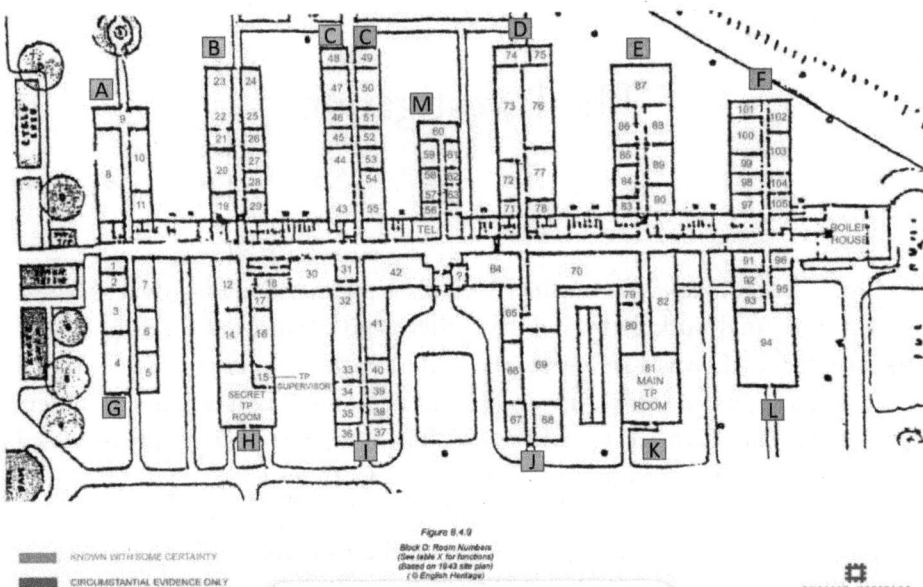

Figure 5: Another Block D site plan, with room numbers added by English Heritage to correspond with a list of the title/purpose of each room. Spur letters (A-M) added by the author. (© *Historic England*)

room, categorising each one as 'known with some certainty' or 'circumstantial evidence only'.[1] They marked all the rooms in Hut 3 as 'known with some certainty', but none as being GBR. So, I did need to try to work it out for myself – essentially by a process of elimination. This felt a bit like a sudoku of rooms!

I started out assuming that the most accurate evidence must surely be Rena's own testimony, as she was there at the time. And yet, Rena's memory was fading when I met her, and once she had died, I couldn't ask her to clarify! I concluded that the best chance of getting to the truth lay somewhere between Rena's recollections and the English Heritage estimates. I also had help from Dr Cheetham, the very obliging Bletchley Park historian with whom I had been corresponding. Let's compare and contrast!

So, Rena described GBR as 'a **great big room**, with typewriters all over the place,' and with '**about 40 people** – all women'. With this in mind, I started scouring the site plans for such a room … until I remembered that Rena had continued: '…but it was **shiftwork**, so we were never all there at the same time'. There were two shifts in operation until February 1945, possibly meaning only about 20 women in the room at a time, and perhaps fewer once the night shift was added. The trouble is, it's hard to locate a room of a particular size on the 1943 site plans because of the changes over time. Partitions might have been added or taken away, for example.

Rena also recounted that '**The three of us were allocated a little side room off the main office**: me, Margery and Elma Morley.' *Right*, I said to myself, *I'm looking for a largish room with a small office attached to it. That should help to narrow it down!* I couldn't go into the building to have a look, but there were a few possibilities on the site plans. Even the *size* of the side room could be useful information. Was it big enough for Rena, Margery and Elma (and their desks), or was just one or two of the friends on duty at a time (so basically a broom cupboard)?! I got the feeling from Rena that they *did* all work together; otherwise, perhaps they wouldn't have developed such a close friendship. Elma's biography indicates that at least she and Rena shared the office, though without any idea of what each other was working on. I do like the idea of all three of them in there together though!

Another factor that might help to pin down the room was that it was, as Rena pointed out, **separated from Hut 3 by a 'corridor'**. This is a bit confusing. I knew that GBR was part of Hut 3 *organisationally* speaking, but might it have been *physically* outside Hut 3? Rena was keeping me on my toes! Could it have been over in Hut 6's area, to the right on the site plans? Or might it not have been in Block D at all, but over in Block G, to the north? GBR did receive its 'bundles of secrets' from 'the Sorting Watch' (a unit which was part of the traffic analysis process), and this was over in Block G. I consulted Dr Cheetham. He said that both of these are unlikely; that GBR wasn't 'attached' to Hut 3 but a 'substantive element of it', and so that's where it would have been located. He added that Rena's good knowledge of Hut 3 and the requirement not to 'wander' mean that it could not have been elsewhere.

Alternatively, the point about separation by corridor could refer to the need to cross from a part of Hut 3 which Rena perceived as 'lesser' to what might be described as the *nerve centre* of Hut 3 (Spur I). This could indicate that GBR was somewhere in Spur C, which was directly opposite I. The English Heritage report claims that GBR would 'undoubtedly' have 'gravitated' towards C.

Strangely for a single-storey building, *steps* also come into it: Rena told me that to get to Hut 3 (though perhaps she just meant to its nerve centre), 'I remember **we went up some steps**, which puzzles me now.' Figure 6 shows that there were a few staircases in the building, but there is no staircase leading from Spur C towards Spur I. And if Rena said there were steps to climb, then steps there were! This rules Spur C out.

The steps actually gave me a bit of a lightbulb moment, though, and for a while, I thought I'd cracked it. I happened to read in the report that Block D sloped upwards from East to West (from right to left on the plan), and I saw the steps leading to Hut 3, shown in the right-hand circle in Figure 6. I thought, *aha! GBR must have been in Room 42.* This was a large room which was actually part of Hut 3; just on the edge. It features an alcove that could have been the small side room, and it would have required going up some steps (right-hand circle) to get to the 'nerve centre'. However, I then read in the report that Room 42 hosted a unit called 'the Backroom Watch' (at least in 1943), so this room might not be a candidate, if the Backroom Watch didn't move somewhere else in 1944. I noticed that the room on the other side of the main entrance (Room 64) was almost a mirror image of 42. Room 64 was marked as 'circumstantial evidence only' on the site plan, so I did wonder about that one, too. But no: this was likely also a dead end: elsewhere in the report it says that Room 64 hosted a unit called 'Air Q-Watch' and was part of Hut 6 (in 1943). I know it's just a room, but I was quite disappointed!

The final piece of evidence from Rena was: 'There was **a window through to the big room**, where we'd get bundles of secrets.' The window might not still be there, but there could be some evidence on site, if only you could go in! It's not clear to me whether by 'the big room' Rena meant a window from the side room to the rest of GBR, or from GBR to the Sorting Watch or elsewhere. If the window looked directly into the Sorting Watch, GBR could only have been in Block G. However, the bundles could have been delivered by hand, as there were messengers whose job it was to take things round the Park. Alternatively, they could have arrived via one of the conveyor belts or pneumatic tubes/chutes that operated in the building. Hence, physical proximity might not have been very important after all.

3

The Conclusion

After all that room sudoku, I'm sorry to report that I failed in my quest. Perhaps we'll never know for sure where the women of GBR toiled away! However, I had one last hope: Dr Cheetham, who came up with a new suggestion. His educated guess was that GBR was actually located in Room 20, over in Spur B, and that Rena's side room might have been Room 19. Room 20 is a good candidate as it was:

- ✓ fairly big;
- ✓ not too far from the 'nerve centre' for Hut 3;
- ✓ the only room in Hut 3 whose purpose was not confirmed in the report (though there are suggestions); and
- ✓ connected to the main corridor by a small flight of steps (left-hand circle in Figure 6).

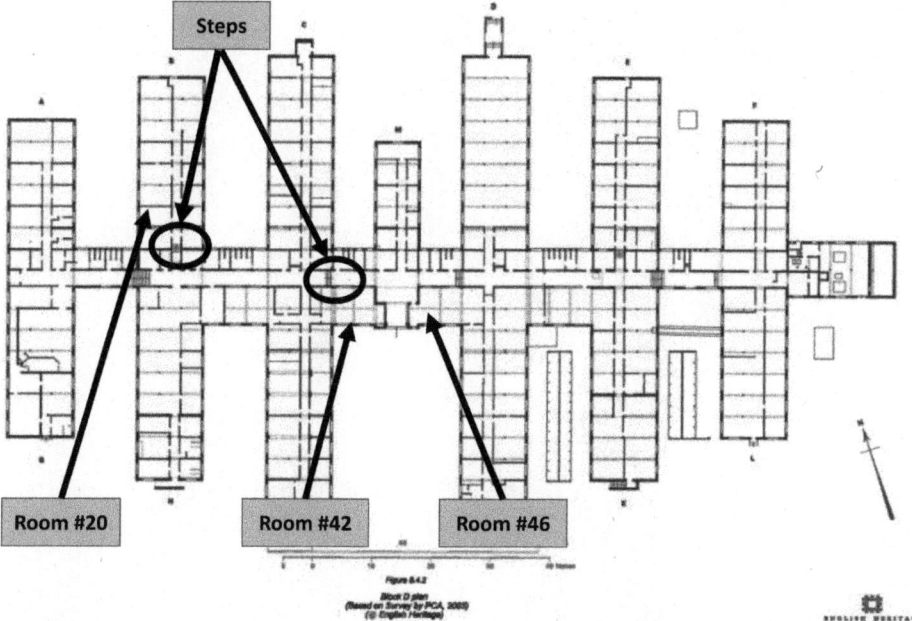

Figure 6: Site plan, showing two staircases of interest (circled) and three rooms of interest. The right-hand staircase went up from Hut 6 into Hut 3. The left-hand one went up from Spur B to the central corridor. (© *Historic England*)

Whether or not this was correct, I hope that Rena will appreciate our efforts, if she's watching. I know that it's just a room, but for the 40 or so 'backroom girls' of GBR it was a significant place, and the work that they did there really mattered. They t*yped for the end of the war (the war)*, and they deserve to be recognised more (and more)!

Mystery Three

Missiles and Monitoring

1

The Mystery

'Rena, did you help solve the Cuban Missile Crisis?' Well, that's what I wish I could have asked her, since something that she'd said had made me wonder. But again, sadly, she died before I could ask. Hence, this became the third mystery. It was a big question to go unanswered, so I decided to try and find out.

Until meeting Rena, I knew very little about this part of history. However, I did know just enough to make the connection in my mind. For the benefit of any other Cuban Missile Crisis beginners like me, the crisis was a confrontation between the United States and the Soviet Union, which took place over 13 days in October 1962. It revolved around the presence of Soviet nuclear missiles in Cuba (90 miles from Florida) and American nuclear missiles in Turkey and Italy. It's considered to have been the closest the world came to full-scale nuclear war during the Cold War.[1] Many people at the time were genuinely afraid that the crisis would lead to the end of the world as they knew it. Scary stuff.

Even some of those more in the know than me might not be aware that the BBC – specifically the staff at Caversham Park – played a significant part in resolving the crisis.[2] In a nutshell, BBC Monitoring (BBCM) acted as the man in the middle, helping to convey vital messages from the Communist Party Leader and head of the Soviet Government, Nikita Khrushchev, to US President Kennedy. Premier Khrushchev used the medium of radio, because this was the fastest method of official diplomatic communication at the time.

To understand exactly what happened, I tried LinkedIn once again. A friend of a friend of a friend (yes, it was a long chain!) put me in touch with Chris Greenway, a BBCM employee, who was kind enough to enlighten me. How it played out was as follows: on Saturday 27 October, Khrushchev announced on Russian radio that he would withdraw his nuclear missiles from Cuba, but only if Kennedy would also withdraw US missiles in Turkey. The BBCM Russia team were ready and waiting, in the Listening Room at Caversham Park. They heard the broadcast and translated, quickly, the main point of what was a rather long message. They then sent this, in a news flash, to the Americans upstairs – the FBIS or Foreign Broadcast Information Service.[3] In turn, the FBIS passed this on to President Kennedy, all within 18 minutes of the original broadcast. This was a huge achievement, given that the previous day a message sent via *diplomatic* channels had taken almost 12 hours to make the same journey. The BBC then broadcast a television news flash to its own audience, a few minutes later.

The crisis was not over yet, because the Americans could not accept these conditions. The next day, a second message from Khrushchev was transmitted, this time within just *three* minutes. This one – which arrived while Kennedy was getting ready to go to church – announced that Khrushchev would indeed back down, without conditions. Without waiting for the rest of the message – instead, just relying on the main point sent by BBCM – Kennedy accepted. The crisis was over. Finally, the BBC Home Service interrupted its programmes with two more news flashes, reassuring the anxious public.

2

The Investigation

So, history lesson over, why might Rena have been involved? Well, because she said that she worked at Caversham Park 'in the early '60s', monitoring Soviet broadcasts (likely among others). However, the exact timing is key, because she actually mentioned the early '60s as being the point at which she finally *left* Caversham, after 10 years, and moved into the newsroom 'back at Bush House'. I haven't been able to confirm the date of her move back to Bush House, but if this was before October '62 then she could not have been *directly* involved, though she might have played some role in further dissemination of the news, from the World Service newsroom. For example, the World Service made a live broadcast of Alistair Cooke's *Letter from America*, which reflected on the crisis.[1] Either way, she would certainly have been *aware* of the crisis, and of Caversham's role. In either location, she would, at very least, have witnessed things suddenly getting very busy!

The second question would be, if Rena *was* working at Caversham in October '62, what particular role might she have played? I realised that this depended largely on which language Khrushchev made his broadcasts in. I did a bit of googling and found that he did these in Russian.[2] So, Rena would not have been involved in receiving and translating these particular messages, because she monitored broadcasts in *English*. Nevertheless, if she were still in the Listening Room, Chris Greenway explained, she would still have been responsible for monitoring any Radio Moscow broadcasts *in English* that followed. These would have presented the Soviet version of events. Chris mentioned that Radio Moscow put a lot of effort into its foreign broadcasts, and that its English service even had targeted versions for different areas. For example, there were separate ones for North America and for Great Britain and Ireland. I'm not sure if Rena also got to use her French and German to monitor foreign language broadcasts as well, but I think not (since she had failed the German Monitor test and German was her stronger language)!

Another way in which I thought that Rena could have been involved was if she had done a stint in the Caversham Newsroom (also known as the News Bureau) before moving back to Bush House *and* was working there during the crisis. Monitors from the Listening Room usually supplied the News Bureau at Caversham with things that they'd just listened to and deemed newsworthy. To understand this set-up better, I consulted the author and journalist Michael (Mick) Smith, who worked at BBCM, with Chris. Mick also happens to have written extensively about Bletchley *and* wrote Rena's obituary for *The Guardian*, so I'm not sure I could have found anyone more perfect! He explained what the News Bureau was:

'*News Bureau* was a rather quaint, historical name for the Caversham Newsroom, dating back to the war. In Rena's time it was very much a newsroom, reporting not just to all BBC news departments but to the major international news agencies, *Reuters, UPI* [*United Press International*]*, AP* [*Associated Press*] and *AFP* [*Agence France Presse*] and, during major crises, also on demand to other media organisations including the newspapers.'

I wondered: if Rena had been employed *there* during the crisis (rather than in the Listening Room), might she have been involved in onward communication of the messages to FBIS, and/or the BBC news flashes to the other BBC departments that followed? The consensus among those I asked is that no, she *didn't* work there. Mick said she had just mangled her words when she once mentioned moving to 'the Caversham newsroom at Bush House' (Caversham and Bush House are two different places).[3] Chris also indicated that the Khrushchev messages went directly to FBIS (bypassing the News Bureau). And apart from all that, Rena spoke disparagingly about the man in charge of the News Bureau. She said: 'The man in charge at the newsroom [and here I believe she meant the News Bureau at Caversham, not at Bush House] thought women were rubbish. One woman got into the newsroom just after the end of the war, and she had a *dreadful* life there! He managed to find fault in her when he wouldn't in a man. I had no ambition to get into *that* kind of newsroom' ... whereas Rena was delighted to move to the Newsroom at Bush House.

3
The Conclusion

In conclusion, I can confirm that Rena wasn't *directly* involved in resolving the Cuban Missile Crisis, but I can't rule out that she might have made some kind of *indirect* contribution. I'd like to think that in one way or another – and even if she just supported her colleagues in the background as it was all going on – Rena once again played her part in history. However, this time it was as a journalist rather than as a soldier, and that is how she wanted to be remembered.

Acknowledgements

Thank you to Rena, and to the following people who helped to piece her story together, as well as those of her three friends, and to investigate the three mysteries:

- Jan Harrison (mutual friend of Rena)
- Stewart Maclennan (Rena's nephew and executor)
- Sally-Anne Thomas (former colleague of Rena) and Juliet Crellin (Sally-Anne's cousin and executor)
- Martin Glynn and Andrea Stone (Agnes' son and granddaughter)
- Ellie Wasmoeth (Elma's daughter)
- Ed Tarwinski and Wanda Drysdale (Margery's son and daughter)
- Amy Jordan and colleagues (Pen & Sword Books Ltd)
- Simon Bragg, Joanna Walsh, Frances Hathorn and Luciana Matone (supportive family/friend proof-readers)
- Dr Thomas Cheetham, Jonathan Byrne, Dean Annison, Iain Standen, Rebecca Foy and Wendy Towler (The Bletchley Park Trust). *20-08-01-14-11-19 18-05-14-01*
- Andrew Whitehead, Ian D. Richardson, Michael (Mick) Smith, Mike Gandon and Chris Greenway (BBC and former BBC staff; some contemporaries of Rena)
- Colonel Nick Fox (formerly of the Intelligence Corps)
- Adam Sisman, E.D.R. Harrison, Blair Worden and Robert Hutton (authors / historians)
- Dauvit Horsbroch (The Scots Language Centre)
- Graham Salter (son of Lionel Salter)
- Peter Wesley (son of Margaret Wesley)
- Revd Sue McCoan, Jamie McCoan and Anne Byfield (St Andrews United Reformed Church, Ealing)
- Linda Monckton, Alyson Rogers and Clare Broomfield (Historic England)
- Paul Johnson and the MoD Access Team (The National Archives, Kew)
- John LeGloahec (*The Text Message* blog, US National Archives)
- Jessica Wiseman and Lydia Healey (University of St Andrews)

- Judith Curtoys (Christ Church College, Oxford)
- Claire Wallace (Suffolk and Cambridgeshire Regiments Museum)
- Owen Fullarton (Military Intelligence Museum, Chicksands)
- 'Bob' and others (MI5 and GCHQ Historical Section)
- Carol Brown and Paul McCue (the Secret WW2 Learning Network)
- Rob Hopmans (World War II Gravestone website)
- Jo Jenkinson and Karen L. Austin BA (Hons) MA (City of Doncaster Archives)
- Graeme Strachan (*The Courier* newspaper, Dundee)
- Bianca Raluca (Snappy Snaps, Farringdon, London)
- Melissa Horsbrough, Reverend John Armstrong and Craig Bond (Wombwell residents).

Notes

Part One: Rena's Story

A splendid Scottish Start to Life
1. This recollection was from an interview that Rena gave in 2014 to Ealing u3a (University of the Third Age), inspired by the BBC radio programme *Desert Island Discs*. In the interview, she talked about her life through the lens of her 'desert island discs': pieces of music that she would want to have with her if she were a castaway on a desert island. The *Gypsy Rondo* (the finale of Haydn's *Piano Trio No. 39 in G major*) was one of her choices. The recording of her talk can be accessed here: youtube.com/watch?v=GGuR-MZXxy0. A performance of the *Gypsy Rondo* can be accessed here: youtube.com/watch?v=317LBGFeds8.
2. This memory was captured in an interview for the BBC, for a three-part programme about the organisation's history – *How the BBC Began*, BBC (2022): bbc.co.uk/iplayer/episode/p0d5w8zv/how-the-bbc-began-series-1-1-accident-and-opportunity, starting at 13:04.

St Andrews: Best Years and Bombs
1. Sources: the bombing of St Andrews in August 1940 and August 1942: fifetoday.co.uk/lifestyle/when-the-bombs-rained-on-st-andrews-1263525; the October 1940 bombing: chaplaincycompanionship.wp.st-andrews.ac.uk/2020/05/11/second-world-war-8-may-2020; and the Clydebank Blitz: wikipedia.org/wiki/Clydebank_Blitz.
2. Source: chaplaincycompanionship.wp.st-andrews.ac.uk/2020/05/11/second-world-war-8-may-2020.

Signing Up: Silk or Khaki?
1. Source: facebook.com/100067774388835/posts/1498188393820840/.

Basic Training: Ranks and Rifles
1. Source: thecourier.co.uk/fp/education/higher-education/1981174/sworn-to-secrecy-the-women-from-fife-and-dundee-who-translated-adolf-hitlers-will/
2. Source: Rena speaking on *Songs of Praise* in 2020: bbc.co.uk/programmes/p08c7q9d.

Officially Secret
1. There have been several Official Secrets Acts in the UK: 1889, 1911, 1920 and 1939, and much later, 1989. The acts of 1911 onwards still apply today. wikipedia.org/wiki/Official_Secrets_Act.
2. Source: facebook.com/100067774388835/posts/1498188393820840/.
3. The Bletchley Park website explains that traffic analysis 'examined the volume, direction, broadcast patterns, call signs and other characteristics of enemy message traffic, rather than the message content.' It continues: 'This information gave vital insight into how

enemy forces were organised and administered, and where they were located.' As the name implies, SIXTA was part of Hut 6. Source: bletchleypark.org.uk/our-story/traffic-analysis/.

Bletchley Beginnings
1. Dr Cheetham says that promotions at Bletchley Park were actually 'frequently to do with bringing military and civilian pay into line, though it's hard to know if that was the case here'.

The German Book Room
1. Sylvia Jane Luxmoore (Westall), a civilian, was a 'Temporary Senior Assistant Officer' at Bletchley, and Head of the German Book Room: bletchleypark.org.uk/roll-of-honour/5714/.
2. Correction thanks to Dr Cheetham, who was referring to the book *The secret war of Hut 3* by John Jackson (Milton Keynes: Military Press, 2002).
3. Dr Cheetham thinks that Rena's statement about 'people who didn't know the Enigma secret' was an assumption, but that it probably wasn't correct. His understanding is that everyone in Hut 3, Hut 6 and SIXTA who needed to consult the books was 'in the know'. But yes, he agrees, they were much more convenient to read than the 'raw' messages.
4. Source: bletchleypark.org.uk/our-story/e144-shark-attack/.
5. I tried and failed to find out what this programme was, but I don't think we're missing out!
6. Field Marshal Albert von Kesselring (1885–1960) – nicknamed 'Smiling Albert' (apparently by his admirers) – was a Luftwaffe officer in the Second World War and one of Nazi Germany's most highly-decorated commanders. wikipedia.org/wiki/Albert_Kesselring. Bletchley Park expert Mick Smith (who wrote Rena's *Guardian* obituary) tells me that Kesselring had been commander-in-chief in Italy for much of the war. Gerd von Rundstedt had been the commander-in-chief West, but as the war came closer to Germany, Hitler replaced him, in March 1945, with Kesselring. Kesselring then toured the front line (the 'tour d'horizon' that Rena referred to).
7. Thanks to Dr Cheetham, Mick Smith and (indirectly) Stephen Fry for helping me to understand the terminology!
8. I came across this helpful way of describing the difference between codes and ciphers in a book by Stephen Fry that I happened to be reading, though the book uses a different example. Stephen Fry *The Liar* (London: Arrow Books, 1997) pp224–225.
9. Source: en.wikipedia.org/wiki/Teleprinter.
10. Mick Smith told me that 'Jelly-fish' was the codename for ciphers used on the link between Hitler and the commander-in-chief West. That would have been von Rundstedt and later von Kesselring (as previously mentioned).
11. Source: Mick Smith, in an email to the author.
12. Source: Mick Smith, in an email to the author.
13. Jackson, John (Ed.) *The Secret War of Hut 3: The first full story of how intelligence from Enigma signals decoded at Bletchley Park was used during World War Two* (Milton Keynes: Military Press, 2002) pp65–66.
14. Jackson *The Secret War of Hut 3* pii.

Park Life

1. Dr Cheetham says that there was a myth that most, or all, of the women at Bletchley Park were Wrens, which Rena seems to have absorbed. He explains: 'The reality was that they were the largest female contingent but never a majority'. Maybe Rena still harboured a wish to join the black silk stocking brigade!
2. Letter provided courtesy of the Bletchley Park Trust.
3. There are very few images of the camp that Rena lived in. However, the Bletchley Park website features a sketch of the camp, by G.H. Gander: bletchleypark.org.uk/our-story/sketches-from-the-archives/.
4. The NAAFI is a British government company, providing recreation, goods and services to service personnel and their families: wikipedia.org/wiki/Navy,_Army_and_Air_Force_Institutes.
5. Hill, Marion *Bletchley Park People – Churchill's Geese that Never Cackled* (Stroud: Sutton Publishing, 2004) pp113–114 and Notes 115 and 116.
6. Another false memory from Rena here – or perhaps she never knew the difference. Nissen huts were 'a prefabricated steel structure, originally for military use, especially as barracks, made from a half-cylindrical skin of corrugated iron' (see wikipedia.org/wiki/Nissen_hut). The huts at the Park were actually Ministry of Works Standard huts, without the curved roof of a Nissen. Dr Cheetham spotted this point and recommended a PhD dissertation which provides descriptions of the numerous different types of huts: Draper, Karey Lee (University of Cambridge): *Wartime Huts: The Development, Typology, and Identification of Temporary Military Buildings in Britain 1914-1945* (2017): repository.cam.ac.uk/items/b4272db6-8f8e-41dd-9a7f-57610c00c75f.
7. *La Mer* by Charles Trenet. Enjoy! youtube.com/watch?v=fztkUuunI7g. The English version is Somewhere Beyond the Sea, by Bobby Darin.
8. A revue is a type of multi-act, popular theatrical entertainment that combines music, dance and sketches: wikipedia.org/wiki/Revue.
9. The beautiful song *Trees*, to which Rena referred, can be heard here: youtube.com/watch?v=vOHekLZD5i4. This is the version by Paul Robeson (though there are others), and I had never heard it until now. What is it about this song that makes me want to cry?! I knew nothing about Paul Robeson, either, but it seems that he was quite a person of note. Born in 1898, he was a black American stage and movie actor, bass-baritone singer, political activist AND professional football player! Here he is in a movie, *Proud Valley*: youtube.com/watch?v=B0bezsMVU7c. The movie is set in a Welsh mine, just before the war, and in it, he gives a special concert for miners. Could he be a candidate for a biographic movie? I think so! Meanwhile, Nelson Eddy was a musician *and* a spy. Wikipedia says: 'Because he spoke fluent German, having studied opera in Dresden during the 1920s, his work as an Allied spy was invaluable until his cover was blown with a near-fatal assignment in Cairo.' Exciting! en.wikipedia.org/wiki/Nelson_Eddy#cite_note-14
10. Thank you to the Bletchley Park podcast for explaining the context! Episode 149 (*Bletchley Park Poetry*) can be heard here: podcasts.apple.com/gb/podcast/e149-bletchley-park-poetry/id550861736?i=1000605120380.
11. A roadhouse was a popular place to eat and drink, a bit like a country pub. For information, see: interwarlondon.com/2021/02/10/6.
12. Elsie Suddaby (1893–1980) was a British lyric soprano: wikipedia.org/wiki/Elsie_Suddaby. Here's an example of her singing (*There were shepherds abiding in the fields* from Handel's *Messiah*, in 1930): youtube.com/watch?v=DMU6gMxbPJ8.

Keeping the Secret

1. Colonel / Group Captain Frederick Winterbotham (1897–1990) published *The Ultra Secret: The Inside Story of Operation Ultra, Bletchley Park and Enigma* in 1974. For information, see: wikipedia.org/wiki/F._W._Winterbotham.
2. Dr Cheetham mentioned to me that the Coventry myth was dismissed by the book *British Intelligence in the Second World War,* by Hinsley et al. He also added that Winterbotham's 'recollections about briefing customers are rather more useful,' but that 'he was writing from memory, and we can identify occasions where he misremembers and misrepresents.'

Demob Deferred

1. Demobilisation was the process of releasing troops from active service. This was a huge challenge at the end of the Second World War: wikipedia.org/wiki/Demobilisation_of_the_British_Armed_Forces_after_the_Second_World_War.

The Epic Journey to Germany

1. J. Lyons & Co. was 'a British restaurant chain store, food manufacturing, and hotel conglomerate'. Their teashops were very popular in the era that Rena is describing. wikipedia.org/wiki/J._Lyons_and_Co
2. The *Ulster Monarch* was originally a passenger ferry, operating between Belfast and Liverpool, from 1929. In WW2, the British military requisitioned the *Monarch*, to serve as an infantry landing ship. Among other things, she transported the SAS to spearhead the invasion of Italy in 1943 (as featured in the 2025 BBC drama, SAS Rogue Heroes, Season Two), took part in the D-Day landings ... and then ferried Rena and co. over to Ostend. A week later, the *Monarch* went home and back to normal service – something for which Rena would have to wait. For more information, see: en.wikipedia.org/wiki/MV_Ulster_Monarch_(1929)
3. *Plattdeutsch* (also known as Low German) is a West Germanic language that is spoken largely in the north of Germany and north east of the Netherlands.
4. To find out about all things shoogly, see this article in *The Scotsman*: scotsman.com/news/scottish-word-of-the-week-shoogle-1563806.

Bad Nenndorf: Back to Work

1. Source: mi5.gov.uk/bad-nenndorf.
2. Agnes MacMorland (married name Chappell) is commemorated on the Bletchley Park Roll of Honour: bletchleypark.org.uk/roll-of-honour/5824/.
3. This according to one of the detainees – Bernd Freytag von Loringhoven. Von Loringhoven was a German officer who was present in the bunker with Hitler. He gave an account of the prison, and of the treatment of prisoners, in his book *In the Bunker with Hitler, The Last Witness Speaks* (London: Phoenix, 2007) p186.
4. Source: wikipedia.org/wiki/Royal_Pioneer_Corps.
5. Macintyre, Ben *Double Cross, The True Story of the D-Day Spies* (London: Bloomsbury, 2012) p35.
6. Colonel Fox quotes an article from the MI5 website: mi5.gov.uk/history/the-cold-war/bad-nenndorf.
7. The 2005 report by *the Guardian* on abuse and neglect at Bad Nenndorf is available here: theguardian.com/uk/2005/dec/17/secondworldwar.topstories3.

A Top-secret Task
1. Source: foreignpolicy.com/2015/04/28/did-the-brutal-death-of-mussolini-contribute-to-hitlers-suicide/.
2. The British National Archives, in Kew, Surrey, contain correspondence between senior British Army officers in relation to Hitler's wills. The treachery of Himmler is mentioned in this correspondence. The correspondence can be found online: *Last will and testament of Adolf Hitler* - catalogue reference WO 208/3779; pp98–99 (labelled 95–96): discovery.nationalarchives.gov.uk/details/r/C4413346.
3. For information on the failed 'Führermuseum' project, see: en.wikipedia.org/wiki/F%C3%BChrermuseum.'
4. Source: Bradsher, Greg (Dr.) *Hitler's final words: His Political Testament, Personal Will, and Marriage Certificate: From the Bunker in Berlin to the National Archives* pp2–3. https://www.archives.gov/files/publications/prologue/2015/spring/hitler-will.pdf
5. The original of Hitler's personal will can be viewed here: catalog.archives.gov/id/6883511?objectPage=2 (US National Archives: *Marriage Certificate, Private Will and Testament of Adolf Hitler*, p.11; Personal Papers of Adolf Hitler; 242: National Archives Collection of Foreign Records Seized; NAID 6883511). The exact articulation of the adjective *kleinbürgerlich* in German can be found on page 10, and a translation (albeit a slightly different one, done by the American military) on page 11.
6. The National Archives, Kew, Surrey, have a translation of the personal will, in the document *Last will and testament of Adolf Hitler* - catalogue reference WO 208/3779; p108 (labelled 105).
7. US National Archives: *Marriage Certificate, Private Will and Testament of Adolf Hitler*, p11; Personal Papers of Adolf Hitler; 242: National Archives Collection of Foreign Records Seized; NAID 6883511. See: catalog.archives.gov/id/6883511?objectPage=11.
8. As mentioned, Hugh Trevor-Roper's book does use 'petty-bourgeois', but not followed by *kleinbürgerlich* in brackets. Rena might have misremembered seeing the latter in the book.
9. Trevor-Roper, Hugh *The Last Days of Hitler* (London: Pan Books, 2012) p156.
10. Trevor-Roper *The Last Days of Hitler* pp159–161.

Life and Love in Post-war Germany
1. The Reichstag (German parliament) fire occurred in 1933, just after Hitler came to power. It was an arson attack, which the Nazis blamed on Communists, and which led the Nazis to impose drastic restrictions on civil liberties. wikipedia.org/wiki/Reichstag_fire
2. The 'cigarette economy' established itself during the war and boomed in post-war Germany: snbchf.com/2023/07/hunt-tooley-cigarette-economy-postwar-germany-1945-48.
3. According to Wikipedia: 'In international economics, the balance of payments … of a country is the difference between all money flowing into the country in a particular period of time (e.g., a quarter or a year) and the outflow of money to the rest of the world.' See: wikipedia.org/wiki/Balance_of_payments.

At the BBC, from the Bottom Up
1. Source: wikipedia.org/wiki/BBC_World_Service.
2. Henrik Ibsen was a Norwegian, modernist playwright and theatre director: wikipedia.org/wiki/Henrik_Ibsen.
3. For more information on Lionel Salter, see: lionelsalter.co.uk.

4. Wikipedia describes Dietrich Fischer-Dieskau (1925–2012) as 'a German lyric baritone and conductor of classical music' and 'one of the most famous Lieder (art song) performers of the post-war period'. Dietrich Fischer-Dieskau - Wikipedia. Here he is, singing *An die Musik*: youtube.com/watch?v=bZZqZTK0FcM.

Caversham Monitoring Station: Progress and Peril
1. Source: bbc.com/historyofthebbc/buildings/caversham-park.
2. Source: bbc.co.uk/iplayer/episode/p0d5w9tb/how-the-bbc-began-series-1-2-building-the-audience (section on Caversham, starting at 34:00).

Into the Newsroom
1. 'Nevertheless, she persisted' is a modern, American feminist slogan, but I thought it quite appropriate for Rena. wikipedia.org/wiki/Nevertheless,_she_persisted
2. *How the BBC Began* (Part 2), starting at 19:56: bbc.co.uk/iplayer/episode/p0d5w9tb/how-the-bbc-began-series-1-2-building-the-audience?seriesId=p0d5w8vz. Northern Rhodesia became Zambia, and Southern Rhodesia, Zimbabwe.

Retirement
1. A *Lied* (plural: *Lieder*) is a German song that sets poetry to music and is performed by a single vocalist and piano: classical-music.com/features/articles/what-are-lieder.

Back to Bletchley
1. Margaret was a founding volunteer, and Tony led the rebuilding of the Colossus code-breaking machine: tnmoc.org/news-releases/2020/3/26/margaret-sale-1932-2020.
2. This video shows Rena, on the right, from 02:47. She couldn't get a word in, other than 'No!': youtube.com/watch?v=PzmTmhM5vtY.
3. Rena gave this commentary during her u3a interview: youtube.com/watch?v=GGuR-MZXxy0, from 42:15.
4. Source: bletchleypark.org.uk/event/from-gccs-to-gchq/.

Songs (and Dances) of Praise
1. Clip from BBC *Songs of Praise* (10 May 2020): https://www.bbc.co.uk/programmes/p08c7q9d [03:06].
2. See/hear Rena's *Desert Island Discs* at: youtube.com/watch?v=GGuR-MZXxy0.
3. Source: standrewsealingurc.org.uk/rena-stewart-at-100. Included with permission from the author of the article, Anne Byfield.

Creature Comforts
1. Rena professed her love of cats during her *Desert Island Discs* talk to u3a (the University of the Third Age), Ealing: youtube.com/watch?v=GGuR-MZXxy0 from 41:11.

... and a Celebration of a Life Well Lived
1. Rena's obituaries in *The Times*, Friday 24 November 2023: thetimes.com/uk/obituaries/article/rena-stewart-obituary-v7x7xjpvt and *The Guardian* (Mick Smith), 5 December 2023: theguardian.com/world/2023/dec/05/rena-stewart-obituary.
2. Rena's Italian obituary, in *La Stampa*, 6 December 2023 (Brava!): lastampa.it/esteri/2023/12/06/news/e_morta_a_100_anni_rena_stewart_lagente_segreto_che_decifro_i_codici_cifrati_dei_nazisti-13913921/.

Part Two: Remembering Rena's Bletchley Friends

Elma Wasmoeth (née Morley)

1. Dr Cheetham believes that Elma's memories about sayings are probably incorrect. He explains: 'Tuning and testing the line would have been done before sending an enciphered message, so the GBR would never see those signals. I believe these sayings would have been used as "padding" to increase security by concealing the true length and the position of predictable elements within the message'.
2. As previously mentioned, the huts at the camp at Bletchley were in fact Ministry of Works Standard huts rather than Nissen huts, but this is how Rena, Elma and perhaps others remembered them.
3. Dorothy Donaldson (married name Benson) is commemorated on the Bletchley Park Roll of Honour: bletchleypark.org.uk/roll-of-honour/2586/.

Margery Tarwinska (née Forbes)
The Mystery

1. This 2021 article by Graeme Strachan in *The Courier* newspaper (Dundee) can be accessed here: thecourier.co.uk/fp/past-times/1981174/sworn-to-secrecy-the-women-from-fife-and-dundee-who-translated-adolf-hitlers-will/?fbclid=IwAR3hJVRxFjsXONjHiEOSnwEmrhy66UYcYHwNP2-hAsDFwqNngoyPE8VuJ3o.

Part Three: Three Mysteries

Mystery One: Bill, Hugh, and Hitler's Wills
The Mystery

1. Hugh Trevor-Roper's Wikipedia page, which includes a mention of the alias 'Major Oughton': wikipedia.org/wiki/Hugh_Trevor-Roper.

Bill

1. West, Nigel *The Friends, Britain's Post-War Secret Intelligence Operations* (Weidenfeld and Nicolson, 1998) contains clues as to Major Oughton's next steps after the war. Nigel West is the pen name of Rupert Allason, author of books and articles on espionage: wikipedia.org/wiki/Rupert_Allason.
2. West, Nigel *The Friends* p70.
3. West, Nigel *The Friends* pp101 and 17 respectively.
4. A Wikipedia page which mentions a William (Bill) Oughton: wikipedia.org/wiki/Security_Intelligence_Middle_East.
5. Bill Oughton is referred to as a 'SIFE officer' by Alexander Nicholas Shaw in *MI5 and the Cold War in South-East Asia: examining the performance of Security Intelligence Far East (SIFE), 1946–1963* (2017): tandfonline.com/doi/full/10.1080/02684527.2017.1289695.
6. Source: secret-ww2.net/resources/soe-special-operations-executive/.

Hugh

1. The GRU is the foreign military intelligence agency of the General Staff of the Armed Forces of the Russian Federation: wikipedia.org/wiki/GRU_(Russian_Federation). The NKVD – People's Commissariat for Internal Affairs – was the interior ministry of the Soviet Union: wikipedia.org/wiki/NKVD.

2. Sisman, Adam *Hugh Trevor-Roper: The Biography* (London: Weidenfeld & Nicholson, 2010), pp158 and 162.
3. Trevor-Roper, Hugh *The Secret World: Behind the curtain of British Intelligence in World War II and the Cold War* (London: I.B. Tauris & Co, 2014), pp1–2 and p36–7. Trevor-Roper explains that there was just one German spy operating in Britain at the start of the war, but that MI5 was controlling him. Adam Sisman explains the early history of RSS and HTR's role in it in his book *Hugh Trevor-Roper, The Biography*, pp77–82.
4. On breaking the *Abwehr* hand-cipher: Max Hastings claims this happened over tea and biscuits; E.D.R. Harrison claims the bathtub. Hastings, Max *The Secret War: Spies, Codes and Guerillas 1939–1945* (London: William Collins, 2016) p58–59; E.D.R. Harrison in the Editor's Introduction to HTR's book *The Secret World*, p2.
5. Worden, Blair (Ed.) *Hugh Trevor-Roper: The Historian* (London: Bloomsbury Academic, 2020) Chapter 7 (Special Service in Germany and *The Last Days of Hitler*) – E.D.R. Harrison, p166.
6. Sisman *Hugh Trevor-Roper: The Biography* p81.
7. Trevor-Roper *The Secret World*, p40.
8. Worden *Hugh Trevor-Roper: The Historian*, Chapter 7 (Special Service in Germany and *The Last Days of Hitler*) by E.D.R. Harrison, p167.
9. Evans, Richard J *The Hitler Conspiracies: The Third Reich and the Paranoid Imagination* (London: Penguin, 2021) p170.
10. Sisman *Hugh Trevor-Roper: The Biography* p133.
11. Sisman *Hugh Trevor-Roper: The Biography* pp132–133.
12. Sisman *Hugh Trevor-Roper: The Biography* p136.
13. Sisman *Hugh Trevor-Roper: The Biography* p133.
14. Worden *Hugh Trevor-Roper: The Historian* Chapter 7 (Special Service in Germany and *The Last Days of Hitler*) by E.D.R. Harrison, pp168–169.
15. Worden *Hugh Trevor-Roper: The Historian*, Chapter 8 ('The Chap with the Closest Tabs': Trevor-Roper and the Hunt for Hitler) by Richard Overy (p200).
16. Trevor-Roper, Hugh *The Wartime Journals* (Ed. Richard Davenport-Hines) (London: I.B. Tauris, 2012), p262.
17. Sisman *Hugh Trevor-Roper: The Biography* p134.
18. Von Loringhoven, Bernd Freytag *In the Bunker with Hitler*, pp185–188.
19. Bradsher, Greg (Dr.) *Hunting Hitler Part VII: The Search Continues, June–September 1945* (2015): text-message.blogs.archives.gov/2015/12/17/hunting-hitler-part-vii-the-search-continues-june-september-1945/.
20. Worden *Hugh Trevor-Roper: The Historian*, Chapter 7 (Special Service in Germany and *The Last Days of Hitler*) by E.D.R. Harrison, p172.
21. Bormann's remains were discovered on a building site in Berlin, in 1972. For information, see: news.bbc.co.uk/1/hi/world/europe/87452.stm.
22. Evans *The Hitler Conspiracies* p168.
23. The Nuremberg trials ran between 20 November 1945 and 1 October 1946.
24. Sisman *Hugh Trevor-Roper: The Biography* p137.

Hitler's Wills
1. Trevor-Roper *The Last Days of Hitler* pxxx–xxi.
2. Trevor-Roper *The Wartime Journals* p274.
3. Details here on Lorenz, Johannmeyer and Zander's missions sourced from *The Last Days of Hitler* by Hugh Trevor-Roper.

4. A translation of Goebbels' appendix to Hitler's political testament is included in the document held at the National Archives, Kew, Surrey: *Last will and testament of Adolf Hitler* - catalogue reference WO 208/3779; p109 (labelled 106).
5. Bormann's rationale for selecting Lorenz is explained in the document held at The National Archives, Kew, Surrey: *Last will and testament of Adolf Hitler* - catalogue reference WO 208/3779; pp98–99 (labelled 95–96).
6. Source: pictureshistory.blogspot.com/2014/09/pichelsdorf-bridge-berlin-hitler-youth-1945.html.
7. A bridgehead is a 'strategically important area of ground around the end of a bridge or other place of possible crossing over a body of water which at time of conflict is sought to be defended or taken over by the belligerent forces.' wikipedia.org/wiki/Bridgehead.
8. Trevor-Roper *The Last Days of Hitler* pp167–168.
9. Trevor-Roper *The Last Days of Hitler* pp195.
10. Trevor-Roper *The Last Days of Hitler* ppxxxi.
11. An MI5 handwriting expert, Captain Skaron, analysed the signatures, as did Hitler's Press Chief, Otto Dietrich, who was in custody. Skaron judged the documents to be genuine; Dietrich declared that as he was *not* a handwriting expert, he could not swear the same. See The National Archives, Kew, Surrey *Last will and testament of Adolf Hitler* - catalogue reference WO 208/3779; pp96–103 (labelled 93–100).
12. The five soldiers were: Herman Rothman (known as Harry) (who later wrote of this moment in his book: *Hitler's Will*), Henry Howard Marcel Roberts (known as Roberts), Peter Blake (formerly Blau), Ralph Parker (known as Parker) and Ernest Alastair Gordon McGarrety (formerly Rummelsburg) (known as Mac). Rothman's book can be bought on Amazon.
13. XXX Corps was a corps of the British Army in World War Two, formed in the Western Desert of Egypt: wikipedia.org/wiki/XXX_Corps_(United_Kingdom).
14. Bradsher, Greg (Dr.) *The Search for Hitler's Political Testament, Personal Will, and Marriage Certificate, Part 1* (2016): text-message.blogs.archives.gov/2016/01/05/the-search-for-hitlers-political-testament-personal-will-and-marriage-certificate-part-i/.

The Investigation
1. Sisman *Hugh Trevor-Roper: The Biography* p139.
2. Bradsher *The Search for Hitler's Political Testament, Personal Will, and Marriage Certificate, Part 1* (2016): text-message.blogs.archives.gov/2016/01/05/the-search-for-hitlers-political-testament-personal-will-and-marriage-certificate-part-i/.
3. Trevor-Roper *The Wartime Journals* p277.
4. Sisman *Hugh Trevor-Roper The Biography* p140.
5. Bradsher *The Search for Hitler's Political Testament, Personal Will, and Marriage Certificate, Part 1* (2016): text-message.blogs.archives.gov/2016/01/05/the-search-for-hitlers-political-testament-personal-will-and-marriage-certificate-part-i/.
6. Bradsher *The Search for Hitler's Political Testament, Personal Will, and Marriage Certificate, Part 1* (2016): text-message.blogs.archives.gov/2016/01/12/the-search-for-hitlers-political-testament-personal-will-and-marriage-certificate-part-ii/.
7. Worden *Hugh Trevor-Roper: The Historian*, Chapter 7 (Special Service in Germany and *The Last Days of Hitler*) by E.D.R. Harrison, p173.
8. Sisman *Hugh Trevor-Roper: The Biography* pp139–140.
9. The National Archives, Kew, Surrey *Last will and testament of Adolf Hitler* - catalogue reference WO 208/3779; pp94 (labelled 91).

10. The National Archives, Kew, Surrey *Last will and testament of Adolf Hitler* - catalogue reference WO 208/3779; p81 (labelled 79).
11. The National Archives, Kew, Surrey *Last will and testament of Adolf Hitler* - catalogue reference WO 208/3779; pp94–95 (labelled 91–92).
12. The National Archives, Kew, Surrey *Last will and testament of Adolf Hitler* - catalogue reference WO 208/3779; p44 (labelled 43).
13. Worden *Hugh Trevor-Roper: The Historian*, Chapter 7 (Special Service in Germany and *The Last Days of Hitler*) by E.D.R. Harrison, pp174–175.
14. The National Archives, Kew, Surrey *Last will and testament of Adolf Hitler* - catalogue reference WO 208/3779; p.74 (labelled 72).
15. The National Archives, Kew, Surrey *Last will and testament of Adolf Hitler* - catalogue reference WO 208/3779; p.46 (labelled 45).
16. Worden *Hugh Trevor-Roper: The Historian*, Chapter 7 (Special Service in Germany and *The Last Days of Hitler*) by E.D.R. Harrison, pp174–175.
17. The National Archives, Kew, Surrey *Last will and testament of Adolf Hitler* - catalogue reference WO 208/3779; p.45 (labelled 44).
18. Trevor-Roper *The Last Days of Hitler* pxxxiv.
19. Sisman *Hugh Trevor-Roper: The Biography* p141.

The Book
1. Trevor-Roper *The Last Days of Hitler* plviii.

The Translation
1. Sisman *Hugh Trevor-Roper: The Biography* p156.
2. Trevor-Roper *The Last Days of Hitler* pxxxiv.
3. Trevor-Roper *The Wartime Journals* p286.
4. The website IMDb lists Rena not as an actress as such, but for her appearance in the documentary *How the BBC Began*, and – of course – on *Songs of Praise*: imdb.com/name/nm10804040/. I have no idea who added her here, nor who created her profile on Wikipedia. Another small mystery!

… and Back to Bill
1. 'MI5 not 9 to 5' was the strapline of the BBC spy drama TV series *Spooks* (2002–2011).
2. West, Nigel (Ed.) *Guy Liddell's Cold War MI5 Diaries, Volumes 2 and 3* (published independently, 2019).
3. West, Nigel (Ed.) *Guy Liddell's Cold War MI5 Diaries, Volume 2*, Kindle version pp16 and 88–89.

Mystery Two: The Missing German Book Room
The Mystery
1. Peter Calvocoressi (head of the Air Section in Hut 3) described the hut as an 'illustrious molehill' in his foreword to John Jackson's book *The Secret War of Hut 3*, pii.
2. The Bletchley Park Trust does have plans to bring the site back into use in some way, but these are longer-term plans only.
3. Linda Monckton, Andrew Williams, Imogen Grundon, Nathalie Barrett and Kathryn Morrison: Historic Buildings Report on Bletchley Park, 2004. Now housed in the Historic England Archive in Swindon: Research report English heritage 3952 (1.1.11/MON). Copyright: Historic England.

The Investigation
1. Monckton et al: Historic Buildings Report on Bletchley Park, 2004.

Mystery Three: Missiles and Monitoring
The Mystery
1. Source: wikipedia.org/wiki/Cuban_Missile_Crisis.
2. The two-part programme *How the BBC Began* explored the role of the Caversham monitoring station in resolving the Cuban Missile Crisis: bbc.co.uk/iplayer/episode/p0d5w9tb/how-the-bbc-began-series-1-2-building-the-audience.
3. The FBIS is now called OSE – The Open Source Enterprise.

The Investigation
1. Alistair Cooke's *Letter from America*, 28 October 1962: youtube.com/watch?v=wYteKH4m1X0.
2. Detail found in a paper by Rosaleen Hughes, Kings College London: *Attention! Moscow Calling: BBC Monitoring and the Cuban Missile Crisis*: iwm.org.uk/sites/default/files/files/2018-11/Attention%21%20Moscow%20Calling%20BBC%20Monitoring%20and%20the%20Cuban%20Missile%20Crisis%20-%20Rosaleen%20Hughes.pdf.
3. I corrected Rena's statement (in Part One) from 'The final job I applied for was for a sub-editor in the newsroom back at Caversham' to '… in the newsroom back at Bush House.'

Bibliography

This book draws on discussions with Rena, her friends, family and former colleagues. It also contains contributions from the families of Agnes, Elma and Margery. Other sources which have been used for the book, or might be of interest, include the following:

Books
Evans, Richard J, *The Hitler Conspiracies: The Third Reich and the Paranoid Imagination* (London: Penguin, 2021)
Fry, Stephen, *The Liar* (London: Arrow Books, 1997)
Hastings, Max, *The Secret War: Spies, Codes and Guerillas 1939–1945* (London: William Collins, 2016)
Hill, Marion, *Bletchley Park People – Churchill's Geese that Never Cackled* (Stroud: Sutton Publishing, 2004)
Hinsley, FH, British Intelligence in the Second World War (London: H.M.S.O., 1993)
Jackson, John, *The secret war of Hut 3: the first full story of how intelligence from Enigma signals decoded at Bletchley Park was used during World War Two* (Milton Keynes: Military Press, 2002)
Macintyre, Ben, *Double Cross, The True Story of the D-Day Spies* (London: Bloomsbury, 2012)
Rothman, Herman (Ed. Helen Fry), *Hitler's Will* (London: The History Press, 2009)
Sisman, Adam, *Hugh Trevor-Roper: The Biography* (London: Weidenfeld & Nicholson, 2010)
Trevor-Roper, Hugh, *The Last Days of Hitler* (London: Pan Books, 2012)
Trevor-Roper, Hugh, *The Secret World* (London: I.B. Tauris, 2014)
Trevor-Roper, Hugh, *The Wartime Journals* (London: I.B. Tauris, 2012)
Von Loringhoven, Bernd Freytag, *In the Bunker with Hitler: The Last Witness Speaks* (London: Phoenix, 2007)
West, Nigel (Ed.), *Guy Liddell's Cold War MI5 Diaries*, Volumes 2 and 3 (published independently, 2019)
West, Nigel, *The Friends: Britain's Post-War Secret Intelligence Operations* (Weidenfeld & Nicholson, 1988)
Worden, Blair (Ed.), *Hugh Trevor-Roper: The Historian* (London: Bloomsbury Academic, 2020)

Academic papers and reports
Draper, Karey Lee (University of Cambridge), *Wartime Huts: The Development, Typology, and Identification of Temporary Military Buildings in Britain 1914-1945* (2017): repository.cam.ac.uk/items/b4272db6-8f8e-41dd-9a7f-57610c00c75f
Hughes, Rosaleen (Kings College London), *Attention! Moscow Calling: BBC Monitoring and the Cuban Missile Crisis* (date unknown): https://www.iwm.org.uk/sites/default/files/images/gallery/Attention%21%20Moscow%20Calling%20BBC%20Monitoring%20and%20the%20Cuban%20Missile%20Crisis%20-%20Rosaleen%20Hughes.pdf

Monckton, Williams, Grundon, Barrett and Morrison, English Heritage, *Historic Buildings Report, Bletchley Park, 2004* (Research Report English Heritage 3952 (1.1.11/MON)). Copyright Historic England.

Articles, blogs and websites

Anon, *Bad Nenndorf: Controversy, Scandal and a Court Martial*, Security Service – MI5 website (undated). Accessed 26 July 2024. mi5.gov.uk/history/the-cold-war/bad-nenndorf

Anon, *Bormann's body 'identified'*, BBC News (4 May 1998). Accessed 26 July 2024. news.bbc.co.uk/1/hi/world/europe/87452.stm

Anon, *Caversham Park: Listening to the world, 1943 to 2018*, BBC.com (undated). Accessed 26 July 2024. bbc.com/historyofthebbc/buildings/caversham-park

Anon, *Chance meeting revealed mum's hidden past*, Dundee Evening Telegraph (18 February 2021). Accessed 26 July 2024. pressreader.com/uk/evening-telegraph-first-edition/20210218/281578063372545

Anon, post about Rena on the Facebook group: Intelligence Corps – The Soldier Behind the Medals (20 December 2015). Accessed 26 July 2024. facebook.com/100067774388835/posts/1498188393820840/

Anon, *Margaret Sale, 1932–2020*, The National Museum of Computing (26 March 2020). Accessed 26 July 2024. tnmoc.org/news-releases/2020/3/26/margaret-sale-1932-2020.

Anon, *Over 4500 Hitlerjugend Boys Fought The Red Army For Days: PICHELSDORF BRIDGE, BERLIN: April 23, 1945*, Pictures History (undated). Accessed 26 July 2024. pictureshistory.blogspot.com/2014/09/pichelsdorf-bridge-berlin-hitler-youth-1945.html

Anon, *Rena Stewart*, IMDb (undated). Accessed 26 July 2024. imdb.com/name/nm10804040/

Anon, *Rena Stewart obituary: First senior female editor for the World Service, and translator of Hitler's will, The Times* (24 November 2023). Accessed 26 July 2024. thetimes.com/uk/obituaries/article/rena-stewart-obituary-v7x7xjpvt

Anon, *Rena Williamson Robertson Stewart*, Bletchley Park website Roll of Honour, including Rena's Oral History project interview (conducted in November 2018). Accessed 26 July 2024. bletchleypark.org.uk/roll-of-honour/8699/

Anon, *Scottish word of the week: Shoogle*, The Scotsman (23 August 2013). Accessed 26 July 2024. scotsman.com/news/scottish-word-of-the-week-shoogle-1563806

Anon, *When the bombs rained down on St Andrews*, Fife Today (27 February 2016). Accessed 26 July 2024. fifetoday.co.uk/lifestyle/when-the-bombs-rained-on-st-andrews-1263525

Arts, Mara, *Roadhouses*, Interwar London (10 February 2021). Accessed 26 July 2024. interwarlondon.com/2021/02/10/6

Bradsher, Greg (Dr.), *Hitler's final words: His Political Testament, Personal Will, and Marriage Certificate: From the Bunker in Berlin to the National Archives*. archives.gov/files/publications/prologue/2015/spring/hitler-will.pdf

Bradsher, Greg (Dr), *Hunting Hitler Part VII: The Search Continues, June–September 1945*, US National Archives' 'The Text Message' website (17 December 2015). Accessed 26 July 2024. text-message.blogs.archives.gov/2015/12/17/hunting-hitler-part-vii-the-search-continues-june-september-1945/

Bradsher, Greg (Dr), *The Search for Hitler's Political Testament, Personal Will, and Marriage Certificate* series of articles, US National Archives' 'The Text Message' website (Part 1: 5 January 2016). Accessed 26 July 2024. Part 1: text-message.blogs.archives.gov/2016/01/05/the-search-for-hitlers-political-testament-personal-will-and-marriage-certificate-part-i/

Byfield, Anne, *Rena Stewart at 100*, St Andrew's United Reformed Church (February 2023). Accessed 26 July 2024. standrewsealingurc.org.uk/rena-stewart-at-100/

Chaudhuri, Lucy, *What are Lieder?* BBC Music Magazine – Classical Music (15 June 2021). Accessed 26 July 2024. classical-music.com/articles/what-are-lieder

Cobain, Ian, *Britain's secret torture centre: The interrogation camp that turned prisoners into living skeletons. German spa became a forbidden village where Gestapo-like techniques were used, the Guardian* (December 2005). Accessed 26 July 2024. theguardian.com/uk/2005/dec/17/secondworldwar.topstories3

The Gerry Holdsworth Special Forces Charitable Trust, *SOE (Special Operations Executive) A Short History, Secret WW2* (undated). Accessed 26 July 2024. secret-ww2.net/resources/soe-special-operations-executive/

Greenway, Chris, Essay for colleagues at BBC Monitoring (not published externally) on the Cuban Missile Crisis, to mark its 60th anniversary in 2022.

Hunt Tooley, T, *To Smoke or Not to Smoke: The Cigarette Economy in Postwar Germany, 1945–48*, Snbchf.com (8 July 2023). Accessed 26 July 2024. snbchf.com/2023/07/hunt-tooley-cigarette-economy-postwar-germany-1945-48

The Lionel Salter Library (website): lionelsalter.co.uk/index.html

Niven, Tracy, *St Andrews and the Second World War*, University of St Andrews Chaplaincy Companionship (11 May 2020). Accessed 26 July 2024. chaplaincycompanionship.wp.st-andrews.ac.uk/2020/05/11/second-world-war-8-may-2020/.

Secret WW2 - The Secret WW2 Learning Network. Accessed 26 July 2024. secret-ww2.net/.

Shaw, Alexander Nicholas, *MI5 and the Cold War in South-East Asia: examining the performance of Security Intelligence Far East (SIFE), 1946–1963*, Taylor & Francis Online (15 February 2017). Accessed 26 July 2024. tandfonline.com/doi/full/10.1080/02684527.2017.1289695

Smith, Michael, *Rena Stewart Obituary, the Guardian* (5 December 2023). Accessed 26 July 2024. theguardian.com/world/2023/dec/05/rena-stewart-obituary

Soloway, Benjamin, *Did the Brutal Death of Mussolini Contribute to Hitler's Suicide?* Foreign Policy (28 April 2015). Accessed 26 July 2024. foreignpolicy.com/2015/04/28/did-the-brutal-death-of-mussolini-contribute-to-hitlers-suicide/

Strachan, Graeme, *Sworn to secrecy: The women from Fife and Dundee who translated Adolf Hitler's will*, The Courier newspaper (17 February 2021). Accessed 26 July 2024. thecourier.co.uk/fp/education/higher-education/1981174/sworn-to-secrecy-the-women-from-fife-and-dundee-who-translated-adolf-hitlers-will/

Whitehead, Andrew, *Witness: Rena Stewart and Hitler's will + TRANSCRIPT*, Andrewwhitehead.net (24 January 2013). Accessed 26 July 2024. andrewwhitehead.net/blog/witness-rena-stewart-and-hitlers-will

WW2 Gravestone website, entry on Wilhelm Zander. Accessed 26 July 2024. ww2gravestone.com/people/zander-wilhelm/.

And many Wikipedia entries, as indicated in the notes to this book.

Radio and podcasts

Episode 149 - Bletchley Park Poetry, Bletchley Park podcast (March 2023). Accessed 26 July 2024. podcasts.apple.com/gb/podcast/e149-bletchley-park-poetry/id550861736?i=1000605120380

Hitler's Will, BBC News World Service 'Witness History' series (25 January 2013) – Rena interviewed by her former colleague Andrew Whitehead. Accessed 26 July 2024. bbc.co.uk/programmes/p0139wkh

Television and videos

Feature: Bletchley Park, BBC Songs of Praise (10 May 2020). Accessed 26 July 2024. bbc.co.uk/programmes/p08c7q9d

How the BBC Began, BBC iPlayer (22 October 2022). Accessed 26 July 2024. https://www.bbc.co.uk/iplayer/episode/p0d5w8zv/how-the-bbc-began-series-1-1-accident-and-opportunity and https://www.bbc.co.uk/iplayer/episode/p0d5w9tb/how-the-bbc-began-series-1-2-building-the-audience?seriesId=p0d5w8vz

YouTube videos (accessed 26 July 2024):
- Rena shares her desert island discs with the Ealing University of the Third Age (u3a), in February 2014: youtube.com/watch?v=GGuR-MZXxy0
- Haydn *Trio No. 39 'Gypsy Rondo', Movement III*: youtube.com/watch?v=317LBGFeds8
- *La Mer*, by Charles Trenet: youtube.com/watch?v=fztkUuunI7g
- The poem *Trees*, by Joyce Kilmer, sung by Paul Robeson: youtube.com/watch?v=vOHekLZD5i4
- Paul Robeson sings to Scottish miners (1949): youtube.com/watch?v=B0bezsMVU7c
- *An die Musik*, by Schubert, sung by Dietrich Fischer-Dieskau: youtube.com/watch?v=bZZqZTKoFcM
- Rena tries and fails to have a chat with Princess Kate at Bletchley Park (2019) youtube.com/watch?v=PzmTmhM5vtY
- Alistair Cooke's *Letter from America*, regarding the Cuban Missile Crisis (October 1962): youtube.com/watch?v=wYteKH4m1X0

Artefacts, letters and diaries

Images of artefacts from Rena's home / estate, including her post-war diary: *FOUR DAYS IN FOUR COUNTRIES - Being an account of the hardships, toils and travails, of a modern Amazon on a trip across battle-scarred Europe* (September 1945)

D'Arcy Wentworth Thompson, museum object details, University of St Andrews Collections (undated). Accessed 26 July 2024. collections.st-andrews.ac.uk/collection/darcy-wentworth-thompson/1004130

Last will and testament of Adolf Hitler (The National Archives, Kew, Surrey) – catalogue reference WO 208/3779

Letter from Margery Tarwinska (née Forbes) from Bad Nenndorf, Germany (September 1945)

Marriage Certificate, Private Will and Testament of Adolf Hitler, p11; Personal Papers of Adolf Hitler; 242: National Archives Collection of Foreign Records Seized; NAID 6883511 (US National Archives)

And various photographs, owners noted in captions if not owned by Rena's nephew.

Index

6 Intelligence School (6IS), 109
21 Army Group, 45, 82
100 years old, 54, 63–7, 69

Ablutions, 23, 43, 75
Abwehr, 35, 87–8
Accommodation,
　at Bletchley Park, 21, 23, 60, 75
　in Ostend, 31
　at Bad Nenndorf, 34, 43
Agence France Presse (AFP), 50, 119
Air Q-Watch, 112
Air Section, 18
Aidenbach, 98
Algeria, 49
Aliases, 45, 63, 82, 85–6, 89–90, 94, 97–8
Allies, 14, 39, 88–90, 94, 98–9
Amateur Dramatics Society (Bletchley Park), 23
Ambition, 3, 26, 47, 52, 55, 119
American Zone (Germany), 92–4, 99
Americans,
　In WW2, 41, 89–3, 96–9, 102
　In the Cold War, 51, 116–117
An die Musik, 49, 62
Anstruther, 71
Appendix to the Führer's Political Testament, 92
Argentina, 88
Armistice Day, 67
Army Index, 11
Associated Press (AP), 119
Atlantic convoys, 15
Auld Lang Syne, 63, 67
Australia, 75
Auxiliary Territorial Service (ATS), 8, 10, 21–2, 29, 32, 34, 71, 74, 77
Axe, 87, 99–100

Backroom Watch, 112
Bad Nenndorf (No. 74 Combined Services Detailed Interrogation Centre), 34–46, 72, 75, 77, 85–6, 89–90, 102, 104–105
Bad Oeynhausen, 41, 89, 92, 96, 102
Baking, 63
Ballroom dancing, 23
Basic training, 9
BBC Empire Service, 48

BBC External Services, 47–8, 53, 55
BBC Home Service, 117
BBC Light Programme, 30
BBC News, 56
BBC Overseas Service, 48
BBC World Service, 40, 47–59, 65, 78, 116–20
　BBC East European Service, 47–8
　BBC European Service, 48
　BBC German Service, 48
　BBC Monitoring (BBCM), 50–2
B.B.S.V., 45
Belgium, 31–2
Berlin,
　Reichstag, 43
　Hitler's bunker, 17, 38–9, 43, 82, 87–90, 92, 94, 96
　Escape attempts, 39, 91–3
　Rena's 'illegal' trip, 43, 75
Berthold, G. (Robert Lucas de Pearsall), 62
Billeting, 60
Birthdays, 26, 63–4
Bletchley Park Girls, 11–29, 47, 60–1, 69, 72, 74–8, 108, 110–12, 114
Bletchley Park
　during WW2, 9–29, 34–5, 38, 41, 44, 46, 60–2, 69–79, 88, 108–14
　post WW2, 27–8, 34, 47–8, 60–2, 64, 75–6, 78, 108, 110, 113, 119
Bletchley Park Trust, museum and staff, 10–11, 14–15, 18, 20–1, 24, 27–8, 60, 110–11, 113
'Blethering', xiii–xiv
Block D, 108–14
Block G, 109, 111–12
Blondi (Hitler's dog), 39
Boats requisitioned by Hitler's messengers, 39, 93–4
'Bob' from MI5, 104–105
Bombes, 15–16
Bombings,
　WW2, 6–7, 28, 31, 33, 43, 87, 93
　IRA, 54
Bormann, Martin, 39, 91, 93, 96, 98
Bottle containing Johannmyer's documents, 100
Brandenburg, 94

'Brass-hats', 98–9
Braun, Eva, 38–9, 42, 90, 93
The British
　In WW2, 10, 18, 29, 33, 35, 41, 82, 88, 92
　Post WW2, 51, 72, 84, 88–91, 94–9, 102
British Army, 8, 10–12, 20, 29–31, 33, 35, 41, 45–6, 60–1, 82, 87, 95, 102, 105
　British Army of the Rhine (BAOR), 29, 45, 82
British Broadcasting Corporation (BBC), 47, 49–54, 58, 64, 68, 116–17, 119
British Museum, 20
British Petroleum, 72
British secret service, 27, 36, 72, 84–7, 90, 104–105
British zone / territory (Germany), 8, 33, 92
Broadcasting House, 50, 58
Brown, Gordon, 61
Broxburn, 74
Bumph Palace, 23–4
Bunker (Hitler's), 17, 38–9, 43, 82, 87–90, 92, 94, 96
Burgdorf, General Wilhelm, 93
Burns, Robert, 63
Burns Suppers, 63
Bush House, 47–9, 52, 54, 58, 118–19
Byrne, Jonathan, 11

Call-up for war service, 8, 9, 72
Calvocoressi, Wing Commander Peter, 18
Camp 020, 36
Canada, 11, 57, 72–3, 75, 77
Canoe, 93
Career, 3, 46–50, 52–6, 65, 72, 75, 78, 84, 87, 89, 97
Carers, 66, 73
Catherine, Princess of Wales (previously Duchess of Cambridge), 61
Cats, 62, 66
Cavalry, 72, 77, 87
Caversham Park, 50–2, 57, 116–20
Cecilia ('Cecil') – surname unknown, 7
Cellardyke, 71
Centenarian / centenary, 54, 63–7, 69
Central Intelligence Agency (CIA), 51, 84
Chain of Command, 10, 98
Charles III, King, 64
Cheetham, Dr Thomas, 10, 15, 18, 27, 60, 110–11, 113
Children, 34, 47, 56, 71–8
Children impacted by WW2, 31–3, 93
Childhood, 3–4, 71, 74, 77
Chopin, Frédéric, 62
Christ Church College, Oxford, 88, 96
Church / Christianity, 9, 62–4, 67, 71–2, 74, 117
　Church of Scotland, 9, 62
　United Reformed Church, 62–4, 67

Churchill, Winston, 24
Cigarettes, 31, 32, 44–5
　Cigarette economy, 44
Cinema, 23, 26
Ciphers / cipher systems, 13–14, 16–17, 87–8
City of Doncaster Archives, 105
Civilians at Bletchley Park, 13, 20, 23, 29, 46, 74
Clerk at the BBC, 47–8
Clydebank / Clydeside bombings, 6–7
Code and code-breaking, 10, 13–18, 27, 49, 61, 72, 74, 88, 108–109
Codebreakers' Wall, 78
'*Codfish*', 17
Coffee, 16, 21, 26
Cold War, 34, 50–51, 116–20
Colossus, 17
Combined Services Detailed Interrogation Centres (CSDIC),
　Bad Nenndorf, 29
　Camp 020, 36
Communism, 91, 104, 116
Concentration camps, 35
Conscription, 5, 8–9
Cooke, Alistair, 118
Corn Exchange (Bedford), 26
Counter Intelligence Corps (CIC), 96
Counter-Intelligence War Room, 88–9
Courses, 9–12
Coventry, 28
Craven "A" Virginia Cigarettes, 44–5
Croatia, 57
Criminals/criminality, 35–6, 44, 77, 86, 96
Cross-country running, 20–1
Crosswords, 67, 77
Cuban Missile Crisis, 51, 116–20
Currency, 26, 30–1, 44
Cyanide, 39, 90, 92
Czechoslovakia, 93

Dancing, 6, 23, 44, 62–4
Dating, 21, 44, 72
D-Day, 17–18
Deciphering, 13–14, 16–17
Decrypts, 11, 13–14, 16, 18
Defence Security Officers (DSOs), 84–5
Degrees, 6–8, 46, 72, 75
Demobilisation, 29, 46, 77, 103
Desert Island Discs, 62–3
Diary, 30–3
Dog (Germany), 44
Donaldson, Dorothy (married name Benson), 75
Dönitz, Grand Admiral (then briefly President) Karl, 39, 92–4
Double Cross, 36
Downfall (movie), 86
Drinking (alcohol), 26, 31, 45, 89, 95

Dublin, 88
Duchess of Cambridge (now Princess of Wales), 61
Duetto buffo di due gatti, 62
Dundee, 77
Dunkirk, 49
Dutch (language and songs), 76
Dutch (people), 32
Duty Editor, 53–4

E Branch (MI5), 105
Ealing, 6, 62–3, 67, 87
East Germany, 48
Eddy, Nelson, 23
Edinburgh (city of), *see also* University of Edinburgh, 6, 71, 74–5, 78
Embankment, 30
Emending, 18
Emigration, 11, 72, 75, 77
Enciphering, 14, 16–17
England, 31, 46, 63, 71–2, 91, 98, 101
English Heritage, 108, 110–11
English (language), 4, 33, 40, 50–1, 57, 76, 118
Enigma, 10, 13–17, 27, 88, 108
Epic journey to Germany, 30–33, 89
Escorts (security at Bad Nenndorf), 35, 44
Europe, 24, 29–30, 72, 89
Exchanging money, 31

Facebook, 69, 105
Fallingbostel prison camp, 94–5
Family,
  Agnes', 71–3
  Bill Oughton's, 105–106
  Elma's, 14, 74–6
  Goebbels', 39
  Hitler's, 38–40
  Margery's, 34, 41, 77–8
  Rena's, 3–6, 11, 27, 30, 45–6, 52, 63–4, 66–7
Fascism, 67
Fashion, 31
Feminism, 12, 52, 54–6, 59, 65, 119
  see also Sexism
Fenchurch Street Station, 30
Festival Hall, 49, 62
Fife, 4–5, 6–7, 67, 71
First World War, 3, 5
Firth of Forth, 4, 71
Fischer-Dieskau, Dietrich, 49, 62
'*Fish*' (code name), 15–17
Fitzjohn's Avenue, 10
Flemish (language), 31
Flensburg, 92–3
'Flinging out' of food (Netherlands and Germany), 32–3

Food, 21, 23, 26, 30–3, 43, 48
  see also Meals
Forbes, Charles and Lilian, 77
Foreign Broadcast Information Service (FBIS) (now OSE – the Open Source Enterprise), 51, 116, 119
Foreign (language) broadcasting, 48, 51, 118
Foreign Office, 37, 48
Four Days in Four Countries, 30
Fox, Colonel Nick, 36–7, 84–6
Frank (surname unknown), 45
Free Polish Army, 77
Freedom of Information Request (Bad Nenndorf), 37
Francs, 31
French (language), 6, 40, 42, 71, 118
French (military / occupation authorities), 91
Friends and friendship,
  Childhood, 4, 77
  St Andrew's, 6–8
  Bletchley Park, 9–11, 14, 20, 23–7, 69, 72, 74–5, 111
  Bad Nenndorf, 34, 41, 45, 75, 77, 82, 86, 89, 102, 104
  BBC years, 46–8, 55, 57
  Retirement, 61–4, 66–7, 76, 78
Friends, The (by Nigel West), 84
Fun, 6, 21, 23–4, 43–5, 49, 54, 57–8, 71–2, 76
Funeral, 67

Gardner, Agnes Ann (née Thomson), 71
Gardner, Martin 'Acorn Mairt', 71
Geldern Ost, 32
General Duties (GD), 43
Gennep, 32
George V, King, 4
George Watson's School, Edinburgh, 74
German (language and sayings), 6, 8, 14, 17–18, 29, 35, 40–1, 44, 58, 71–2, 74, 87, 95, 118
German Book Room (GBR), 10–11, 13–19, 24, 60, 74, 77, 108–14
German Jewish soldiers, 35, 41, 95–6
German military, 13–18, 32, 34, 72, 74, 86, 88–9
  Army, 10, 13, 35, 72, 87–8, 90, 93
  Luftwaffe, 6–7, 13, 28, 39, 87
  Navy, 10, 15, 39, 92–4
German police, 98
German women at the end of WW2, 35
Germany,
  During WW2, 48, 87
  Post WW2, 29–30, 32–48, 72, 75, 77, 79, 82, 84, 88–9, 96, 98, 102, 105
Gill, Walter, 87–8
Glass ceilings, 56
Glass fragments in library books, 7

Glavnoje Razvedyvatel'noje Upravlenije (GRU), 86
Glen Lyon, 4–5, 77
Glynn, Agnes ('Aggie') (née Gardner), 8–9, 11, 14, 69, 71–3, 75–6
Glynn, Hubert, 72
Glynn, Martin, 71–2
Goebbels, Joseph, 38, 92
Göring, Hermann, 39
Going Bush in Bletchley, see Pocock, Michael
Government Code and Cypher School (GC&CS), 61
Government Communications Headquarters (GCHQ), 61
Graduation, 6, 8, 71
Gramophone, 23
Grandchildren (Agnes'), 72–3
Great British Bake Off, 63
Greenway, Chris, 116, 118
Guardian, the, 37, 67–8, 119
Guildford, 9
Gypsy Rondo, 3, 62

Hague, The, 76
Hampstead, 10
Hand-cipher, 87–8
Hanover, 34, 43–4, 94
Happiness,
  Childhood, 4, 74
  St Andrews, 6, 74
  Bletchley Park, 15, 21, 23
  Bad Nenndorf, 31, 43, 44–5, 75
  BBC years, 49, 52, 54, 57
  Retirement, 24, 58, 64, 73
Harris Academy, Dundee, 77
Harrison, E.D.R., 90, 99
Harrison, Jan, 61, 66
Haydn, Joseph, 3, 62
Himmler, Heinrich, 39
Historic Buildings Report on Bletchley Park, 108, 110
Historians, 10–11, 13, 15, 18, 27–8, 42, 60, 87, 89–91, 99, 104, 108, 110–11, 113
History, 36, 41, 45, 51, 79, 82–4, 87–8, 98, 101, 104, 106, 108, 116, 120
Hitchcock, Alfred, 86
Hitchhiking, 26, 72, 75
Hitler, Adolf,
  WW2, 15, 17, 21, 43, 48
  Marriage, 39, 93, 95
  Suicide, 38–9, 42, 82, 86, 88–9, 90–91
  Wills, 38–42, 46, 77–8, 82–103
Hitler Youth, 93
Hoch, Ján (later known as Robert Maxwell), 96
Holidays, 4, 57–8, 77
Holland / Netherlands, 14, 32, 76

Honeymoon (Rena's parents), 4
Honours degrees (and not having one), 7–8, 46
Hopkins, Harry, 88
Horrocks, Lt General Brian, 95
Horse riding, 72, 97
Hotel Leopold (Ostend), 31
Housewife (and not wanting to be one), 3, 26
How the BBC Began, 51, 53
Hugh Trevor-Roper: The Biography, 82, 86, 89–90, 102
  see also Sisman, Adam
Hummerich, Corporal, 93
Humour, 20–1, 23–4, 30, 43–5, 54, 58, 62, 75
Huts at Bletchley Park, 20
  Hut 3, 10–11, 13–19, 27–8, 88, 108–14
  Hut 6, 13, 18, 28, 111–12
  Hut 8, 108
  Accommodation huts, 23, 43, 72, 75
Hutton, Robert, 104
Hyde Park, 30

Ibarra, Vilma, 73
Ibsen, Henrik Johan, 48
'Illustrious molehill', 18, 108
IMDb, 103
In the Bunker With Hitler, 90
  see also von Loringhoven, Bernd
Inca trails, 57
Inquiry (Bad Nenndorf), 36–7, 104
Intelligence,
  British military (WW2), 10–11, 13–15, 18, 29, 36, 41–2, 46, 61, 71–2, 77, 82, 84–8, 90, 95–6, 98–9, 102, 105, 109
  British miliary (Post WW2), 29, 36, 41–2, 46, 51, 72, 77, 82, 84, 86–8, 90, 95–6, 98–9, 102, 105
  British secret service, 27, 36, 49, 51, 61, 72, 84–6, 87–8, 98, 102, 104–105
  German, 34–5, 72, 87, 89
  American, 41, 51, 96, 84, 99
  Russian, 86
Intelligence Corps, 14, 29, 36, 41, 44, 46, 77, 82, 84–5, 95, 99, 102, 105
Interrogation, 29, 34–6, 43, 75, 86, 89–90, 95–8
Irish Republican Army (IRA), 54
Iserlohn, 96, 99–100
Italy, 20, 39, 67, 116

Jackson, John, 18
'*Jelly-fish*', '*Octopus*' and '*Squid*', 17
Jews, 35, 39, 41, 95–6
  Jewish soldiers in the British Army, 35, 41, 95–6
Job-hunting, 46–50, 52–5, 65
Johannmeyer, Major Willy, 93–6, 99–100

Joint Intelligence Committee (JIC), 98–9, 102
Jones, Gwyn, 55
Journalism,
  Early aspirations, 6, 26, 30
  Sexism/feminism, 12, 52, 54–5, 65
  Career progression, 49–50, 52–6, 58, 65
  Techniques and responsibilities, 48, 50–5, 58–9
  News agencies, 50, 119
  News stories, 37–8, 98
Judy the cat, 66
Junge, Gertraud 'Traudl', 39

Kemp, Senior Commander ED, 21, 36
Ken the editor (surname unknown), 54
Kennedy, President John F., 116–17
Khaki (in ATS uniforms), 8
Khrushchev, Nikita Sergeyevich, 116–17
Kilmer, Joyce, 23
Kit (army), 30–1
Kleinbürgerlich, 40–2
Korean War, 51

La Mer, 23, 62,
Languages, dialects and accents, 6, 47–9, 51, 57, 74, 77, 118
  French, 6, 40, 42, 71, 118
  German, 6, 8, 13–14, 18, 29, 34–5, 38, 40–2, 44, 58, 63, 71–2, 74, 77, 83, 87, 95, 99, 101–103, 118
  Flemish, 31
  Plattdeutsch, 32
  Russian, 91, 116, 118
  Scots, xiii–xiv, 4, 31, 33
Largo Parish Church, 67
Last Days of Hitler, The, 41–2, 77, 86, 97, 101–103
  see also Trevor-Roper, Hugh
Laud, Archbishop of Canterbury William, 87
Leon, Sir Herbert, 20
Lethbridge, Major General J.S., 98–9
'Letter' (academic certificate), 6
Letter From America, 118
Letter from Gordon Brown, 61
Letter from King Charles, 64
Letter from Margery to Agnes MacMorland, 34–5, 43, 45
Library at St Andrews University, 7
Liddell, Guy, 104
Lieder, 58, 63
LinkedIn, 69, 104, 116
Linz, 39
Listening Room (Caversham Park), 116, 118–19
Living conditions, 21, 23, 43, 72
Log reading, 10

London, 4
  WW2, 10, 26, 72, 75, 87–8
  Bad Nenndorf / Hitler investigations, 30, 95, 98–9
  BBC years, 46, 48–51, 57, 63, 67, 72, 78, 87, 105, 118–19
  Retirement, 58, 62
London Gazette, The, 85
Lorenz (cipher system), 15–17
Lorenz, Heinz (alias Georges Thiers), 92–6
Lott, Felicity, 63
Love note to Rena, 45
Lower Largo, 77
Luftwaffe, 6–7, 13, 28, 39, 87
Lundin Links, 4, 77
  Lundin Mill Public School (now Lundin Mill Primary School), 4
Luxembourg, 94
Luxmoore, Jane, 13
Lyons, 30

Macintyre, Ben, 36
Mackie, Jean, 57
Maclennan, Isabella 'Isobel' (née Stewart), 3, 6, 63, 66
Maclennan, Stewart, 30, 63–4
MacMorland, Agnes (married name Chappell), 34, 43
Mail motor, 4
Make me a channel of your peace, 62
'Man position', the, 6, 44–5, 56–7
Mansion (Bletchley Park), 20, 61, 108
Marathon, Ontario, 72
Marks (German *Reichsmarks*), 31, 44
Marriage (and not getting married), 3–4, 11, 14, 26, 34, 47, 56, 72, 75, 77
  Hitler's marriage, 39, 93, 95
Mathers, Hugh, 62
Matriculation, 8
Meals, 21, 26, 30–3, 43, 76–7
  see also Food
Medals, 61
Media, 6, 12, 26, 30, 37–8, 49–50, 52–6, 58–9, 65, 67, 77, 88, 91, 94, 96–9, 104, 116–20
  see also Journalism
Mein Kampf, 21
Mein Kemp, 21
Memories, 4, 6, 9–10, 13, 18, 20, 23–4, 26, 39–40, 43–4, 49, 53–4, 57, 62, 64, 76, 77, 111, 120
Memory loss / misremembering, 3, 11, 16, 21, 36, 38, 47, 53, 57, 64, 67
4, 6, 9–11, 13, 16, 18, 20–1, 23–4, 26, 36, 38–40, 43–4, 47, 49, 53–4, 57, 62, 64, 67, 102, 110–11
'Men's jobs', 56
Merrill, Robert, 23

Messengers tasked with transporting Hitler's wills, 39, 92–100
Mexico, 57
MI5, 36, 72, 84–5, 104–105
MI6, 84, 86–7
MI8, 10, 87
Middleton, Kate (Catherine, Princess of Wales), 61
Military discipline, 20–1
Military Index, 11
Miller, Glen, 75
Minden, 33, 86
'Modern Amazon', 30
Monitoring (BBCM), 50–2, 116–20
Montgomery, Field Marshal Bernard, 45
Montreal, 72
Moray House School of Education and Sport, Edinburgh, 75
Morgan Academy, Dundee, 78
Morgen!, 63
Morley, Elisabeth 'Bessie' (née Miller), 74
Morley, James, 74–5
Morse code, 14, 16
Munich, 93, 96–7
Music, 3–4, 23–4, 26, 31, 48–9, 58, 62–3, 76, 108
Mussolini, Benito, 39
My bonnie lies over the ocean, 24
Mystery men, 6, 26, 45

Naródnyj komissariát vnútrennix dél (NKVD), 86
National Archives (UK), 41, 85, 98
National Archives (USA), 41, 97
National Union of Journalists (NUJ), 50
Navy, Army and Air Force Institute (NAAFI), 21, 30–1
Navy (Royal), 8, 20, 61, 71
Nazism / National Socialism,
 WW2, 35, 36, 39, 42, 50, 67, 87
 Post war, 34–5, 77, 88, 93, 97, 99
Netherlands, 32, 76
New Statesman, The, 103
News agencies, 50, 55, 119
News Bureau (Caversham), 50, 52, 118–19
News flashes, 116–17, 119
Newsrooms, 26, 50, 52–5, 58–9, 118–19
Night watch, 13
Nightmares, 27
Nissen Huts (or rather, Ministry of Works Standard Huts), 23, 43, 75
No. 1 War Criminals Holding Centre, Minden, 86
No. 74 Combined Services Detailed Interrogation Centre (No. 74 DIC), 34
Non-Commissioned Officers (NCOs), 34–6, 47

Nonconformists, 9
Northern Rhodesia, 53
 see also Southern Rhodesia
Nuclear missiles / war, 116
Nuremburg Trials, 91, 103

Obituaries, 67–8, 119
Official Secrets Acts, 8, 10, 78
Ohio, 77
Ontario, 11
Ostend, 31–3
Ottawa, 72
Oughton, Harry and Margaret, 105
Oughton, Major John, 84–5, 105
Oughton, Major William ('Bill') Hirst, 34, 38, 40–1, 82–6, 89–90, 102, 104–106, 108
 see also Trevor-Roper, Hugh
Oxford (city of), 75
 see also University of Oxford

Paddington Station, 30
Parents,
 Rena's, 3–6, 27, 45, 52, 67
 Agnes', 71
 Elma's, 74–5
 Margery's, 77
Parades (military), 9, 30
Parey, 94
Parties, 23, 45, 64, 75, 78
'Paustin, Friedrich-Wilhelm', 97–8
 see also Zander, Wilhelm
Pay (BBC), 50
Peace, 21, 29, 58, 62, 67
Peden, Mima, 74
Perth, Australia, 75
Perthshire, 4
Petty-bourgeois, 40–2
Pfaueninsel, 93
Photographs, 44–5, 57, 69, 78, 105, 108
Physical Education (PE), 21, 30, 69
Piano-playing, 3, 49, 58
Plattdeutsch, 32
Ploen castle, 89
Pocock, Michael, 20
Poetry, 6, 21, 23, 58, 74, 76
Postcards from Germany, 44–5
Potsdam, 94
Press conferences, 99
Pride in one's achievements, 3, 11, 27, 30, 41, 52, 59, 65, 69, 78
Prisoners of war, 32, 34–7, 72, 75, 86, 90–1, 96
Privacy (regarding relationships with the opposite sex), 6, 26, 45
Promotion (at work), 11, 29, 48, 50, 52–3, 54, 104
Propaganda, 48

Pseudonyms, 45, 63, 82, 85–6, 89–90, 94, 97–8
Punting, 75
Purity Patrol ("P" Patrol), 21

Quadripartite Intelligence Committee, 90, 98

Racketeering, 44
Radio France, 49
Radio Moscow, 51, 118
Radio Newsreel, 52
Radio Security Service (RSS), 87
Radio traffic / analysis, 10, 16, 18, 60, 109, 111
RAF Fayid, Egypt, 84
Ramsbotham, Major Peter, 98
Rank (and ignoring it), 10–11, 20, 27, 29, 48, 74, 84–5, 104
Ravelston (Edinburgh), 78
Reading (city), 50
Recreation, 4, 6–7, 20–6, 31, 43–5, 49, 57–8, 62–3, 71–2, 74–7
Red Army, 38–9, 93
Redpath, Jean, 63
Refugees, 31, 35, 48
Reichstag, 43
Reid, Captain John Rollo, 95
Research, 82–4, 89, 108
Retirement, 52, 58–66
Reuters, 50, 119
Revues, 23
Rheine, 33
Richardson, Ian D., 55
Rifle training (with a broomstick), 9
River Elbe, 94
River Havel, 93
River Rhine, 33
Roadhouses, 26
Robeson, Paul, 23
Roosendaal, 32
Route marches, 21
Royal Air Force (RAF), 20, 26–7, 84
Royal Albert Hall, 49
Royal Army Medical Corps (RAMC), 31
Royal Festival Hall, 49, 62
Royal Navy, 8, 20, 61, 71
Royal Pioneer Corps, 35
Rumours about Hitler's fate, 88–9, 91
Russia, 34, 38–9, 43, 51, 57, 75, 86, 88–91, 94, 96, 99, 116, 118
Russia desk (Caversham Park), 51
Russian (language), 118
Russian Zone (Germany), 43, 75, 93

Sabbatical, 57
'*Sägefisch*' ('Sawfish'), 17
Sale, Tony and Margaret, 60
Salter, Graham, 49

Salter, Lionel, 48–9
Sanderson, Colonel LHF, 99
Sands, Colonel, 99
Scherzo No. 2 in B-Flat Minor Op. 31, 62
Schörner, Field Marshal Ferdinand, 93
School, 3, 4, 6, 71, 74–7
Schrift, 39
Schutzstaffel (SS), 35, 93, 98
Scotland, 3–7, 17, 29, 46, 67, 71–2, 74–5, 77–8
Scotland Yard, 54
Scots language and accent, xiii–xiv, 4, 31, 33
Scots Language Centre, 4
Scottish dancing/culture and Scottishness, 6, 23, 62–4, 66, 76
Scottish Oil, 74
Sean the NCO (surname unknown), 35–6, 47
Seaplane, 93
Seasickness, 31
Seaside, 31, 64
Second World War and its aftermath, 6–46, 48, 50, 82–106, 108–14
Secret Intelligence Service (SIS), 27, 72, 84–7, 90, 104–105
see also Intelligence, MI5, MI6,
Secret enemy messages, 10– 11, 13–18, 72, 74–5, 87–8, 109, 116, 118–19
Secret Service, 36
Secrecy,
    WW2 / Bletchley Park, 9–11, 14–16, 18–19, 27–8, 46, 61, 72, 78, 87–8, 111–12
    Post WW2, 38, 41–2, 46, 84, 86, 90, 95, 99, 102–103, 108
    Caversham Park, 50–1
Security risk in post-war Germany, 32, 34–5, 44
Security Intelligence Far East (SIFE), 84–5, 104–105
Security Intelligence Middle East (SIME), 84–5, 104–105
Security Liaison Officers, 84
Senior Duty Editor (SDE), 54–5, 59, 62, 65
Sergeant / Sgt McHaggis, 45, 63
Sergeant's Mess,
    at Bletchley Park, 23, 75
    at Bad Nenndorf, 43, 45
Service (to the nation), 8, 20, 45, 61, 64, 68, 104–105
Service hostels, 26
Services, the, 29
Sexism, 12, 52, 54–6, 59, 65, 119
    see also Feminism
Shakespeare, 48
'*Shark*' blackout, 15
Shenley Road Military Camp, 21, 23
Shiftwork, 13, 17, 19, 23, 26, 54, 75, 110
Shoogly / Shoogly bridge, 33

Shorthand, 3, 12
Shredded Wheat, 64
Side room in GBR, 14, 111–13
Sightseeing, 45
Signals intelligence, 10
Silk (in Wrens' uniforms), 8
Sisman, Adam, 82, 86, 89, 90, 102
Six Traffic Analysis (SIXTA), 10, 18
Sleighing, 45
Sleuthing, 69, 79, 104, 108
Smith, Mick, 119
Snowbirding, 72
Social life, 4, 6–7, 20–6, 31, 43–5, 49, 57–8, 62–3, 71–2, 74–7
Songs of Praise, 62
Sorting Watch, 10, 111–12
Soulbury, 14
Southern Rhodesia, 53
  see also Northern Rhodesia
Soviet Union, 34, 39, 43, 51, 57, 75, 86, 88–91, 93–4, 96, 116, 118
Space race, 51
Special Operations Executive (SOE), 84
Spider block, 109
Spies and spying, 23, 36, 72, 83–7, 104–105
Sports, 20–1, 24–6, 30, 72, 77, 69
Spur B, 109, 113
Spur C, 109, 111
Spur I, 109, 111
Sputnik, 51
St Andrew's United Reformed Church, Ealing, 63–4, 67
St Andrews (city of), *see also* University of St Andrews, 6–7, 71
St Francis of Assisi, 62
St Mary's Church Perivale, 64
Stampa, La, 67
Stalin, Joseph, 51, 88
Stars and Stripes newspaper, 99
Stephens, Lieutenant Colonel Robin 'Tin Eye', 36–7, 90, 104
Steps / staircases (Hut 3), 13, 111–13
Stewart, Andrewina ('Reenie' / 'Rena'), 3–4, 52
Stewart, Thomas Robertson, 3–5, 67
Stewart Society, 63
Stockings, 8, 75
Stone, Andrea, 71
Strachan, Graeme, 77
Strand, The, 54
'Strange tribe' of Bletchley Park, 20–1
Strauss, Richard, 63
Stroupach, 4
Sub-editor, 52–4
Sudaby, Elsie, 26
Suffolk Regiment and Suffolk Regiment Museum, 85, 104–105

Surrey, 9, 36, 72
Suez crisis, 51
Swan Song of G.B.R., The, 24, 108
Swimming, 31, 72, 77
Switzerland, 39

Tanks (military), 72, 77, 87
Tapestry Independent Living Home, 73
Tarwinska, Margery (née Forbes), 69
  Childhood, 77
  St Andrew's university, 77
  Bletchey Park, 11, 14, 24, 75, 77, 111
  Bad Nenndorf & Hitler's will, 31, 34–5, 38, 40–5, 77, 82–3, 87, 89, 92, 95, 99, 101–103
  Later life, 77–8
Tarwinska, Rena, 78
Tarwinski, Edmund 'Ed', 34, 77–8
Tarwinski, Marian Jozef, 77
Tashkent, 57
Teaching (and not wanting to be a schoolteacher), 3, 6, 75, 77
Tegernsee, 97–8
Telegraph Room, 61
Teleprinters, 16–17, 50
Temple Meads station (Bristol), 30
Templer, Major General GWR, 98
Tennis, 24, 26, 72
Territorial Army, 87
Text Message, The, 97
Theatre, 23, 26, 48, 57–8, 86
'Thiers, Georges', 94
  see also Lorenz, Heinz
Thomas, Sally-Anne, xi–xii
Thompson, Professor D'Arcy Wentworth, 7
Three ranks, 9, 21
Tilbury Docks, 30
Times, The, 58, 67, 68
Tour d'horizon, 16
Traffic analysis, 10, 18, 109, 111
Training, 9–11, 30, 52, 72, 75
Translation, 13–14, 34, 38, 40–2, 49, 77, 83, 87, 95, 99, 101–103, 116, 118
Transport / methods of transport, 43, 61
  American jeep, 98
  bicycle, 77
  canoe, 93
  car, 89, 98, 100
  coal lorry, 26
  plane, 39, 89, 91, 93, 96
  seaplane, 93–4
  train, 26, 30, 32–3, 45, 89
  tram, 31
  truck, 31, 39, 94
  yacht, 39, 93
Travel, 30–3, 43, 57–8, 89, 91, 96
Trees (poem and song), 23

Trenet, Charles, 23, 62
Trevor-Roper, Hugh Redwald (later Baron Dacre of Glanton),
  Pre-war, 87
  WW2, 87–8
  investigation into Hitler's fate, 42, 82, 86, 89–91
  investigation into Hitler's wills, 82, 86–7, 92, 96, 104
  The Last Days of Hitler, 41–2, 77, 86–7, 97, 101–103
  Hugh Trevor-Roper: The Biography, 89–90, 102
Trio in G, 3
Truscott, General Lucien King, 99
'Tunny', 15, 17
Turing, Alan, 14
Tusa, Sir John, 53
'Two million surplus women' of World War One, 3, 47
Typing, 3, 11–16, 18, 24, 34, 39, 40, 46–8, 69, 74–5, 102, 110, 114

U-Boats, 15
u3a (University of the Third Age), 62
Ulster Monarch, 30
'Ultra', 13, 27–8, 72
Ultra Secret, The, 27
Uniform, 8, 20, 45, 75
United Kingdom (UK), 29, 36, 46, 57, 104
United Press International (UPI), 119
United Reformed Church, 62–4, 167
United States,
  In WW2, 41, 89–93, 96–9, 102
  In the Cold War, 51, 116–17
United States military, 41, 89, 91–3, 96–7, 99, 102
  United States Third Army, 99
University of Edinburgh, 6, 74–5
University of Oxford, 87–8, 90, 96, 101–102
University of St Andrews, 6–9, 71, 77
Unterholzner, Ilsa, 98
Unterholzner, Irmgard, 98
Uphall, 74
Uzbekistan, 57

Vancouver, 11, 72–3
Vet in Germany, 44
Victory in Europe Day (VE Day), 24
Victory in Japan Day (VJ Day), 23
Vilshofen, 97–8
Volunteering for war, 5, 8, 71–2, 74, 77, 87

Von Kesselring, General Field Marshal Albert, 15–16
Von Loringhoven, Bernd Freytag, 90

Waid Academy, Anstruther, 71
Wannsee, 93
War criminals, 35, 77, 96
War Office, 87
War Officer Selection Board (WOSB), 29
Warrington, 106
Washing machines, 26
Wasmoeth, Ellie, 74, 76
Wasmoeth, Elma 'Sunshine' (née Morley), 11, 14, 24, 60, 69, 72, 74–6, 78, 111
Wasmoeth, Ton, 75–6
Weiss, Agent Arnold Hans, 96–8
Wesley, Margaret, 57
Wesley, Peter, 11
West Germany, 48
West, Nigel (Rupert Allason), 84–5
Wheelie suitcase, 57
White, Sir Dick, 88–9, 101–102
Whitehead, Andrew, 58
Wikipedia, 82, 84
Windmill Road (Wombwell), 105
Winterbotham, Group Captain Frederick, 27–8
Winter, Lidine, 66
Wireless, 4, 87–8
Witnesses (to Hitler's fate, and for the Nuremburg Trials), 89–91
Wombwell, 105–106
Women journalists, 52, 55–6, 59
'Women's jobs', 12
Women's Auxiliary Air Force (WAAF), 20
Women's Fellowship, 15
Women's Institute, 15
Women's Royal Naval Service (Wrens), 8
World War One and its aftermath, 3, 5
World War Two and its aftermath, 6–46, 48, 50, 82–106, 108–114
Wormwood Scrubs Prison, 87

XXX Corps, 95

Yacht, 39, 93
'Yellow press', the, 99

Zander, Wilhelm (alias Friedrich-Wilhelm Paustin), 93–9
Zhukov, Marshal Georgy Konstantinovich, 88